REFORM'D

REFORM'D

BREAKING THE CYCLE OF MASS INCARCERATION

TINKA RANDLE

REFORM'D

BREAKING THE CYCLE OF MASS INCARCERATION

CHOSEN MEDIA PRODUCTIONS

REFORM'D: BREAKING THE CYCLE OF MASS INCARCERATION

All rights reserved © 2018 by Tinka Randle

No part of this book may be reproduced or transmitted in any form or by any means, graphic, electronic, or mechanical, including photocopying, recording, taping, or by any information storage retrieval system, without the written permission of the publisher.

Author: Tinka Randle

ISBN-13: 9780578448466

LCCN: TBD

Contact Tinka Randle

Social Media

Facebook – Tink Randle
Instagram - @MsTink1

Email

reformdforever@gmail.com

Table of Contents

Acknowledgments 2
Dedication 6
Chapter 1 – The Meeting 8
Chapter 2 – Baby and His Lady 31
Chapter 3 - Lost Girl 52
Chapter 4 – I Was Locked Up, Too 72
Chapter 5 – A Chance for New Life 128
Chapter 6 – Desperate Times, Desperate Measures 153
Chapter 7 – Mentally Preparing for Bid Number 2 179
Chapter 8 – Breaking Free 206
EPILOGUE 236
STATISTICS 256

Leviticus 26: 23 – 24 KJV" *And if Ye will not be <u>Reformed</u> by me these things, but will walk contrary unto me; Then I will also walk contrary unto you, and will punish you yet seven times for your sins."*

Acknowledgments

I would first like to give my praise, attention, gratitude, and love to The Most High. Thank you Father for using a painful life changing event in my life that turned into my purpose! I'm humbled that you chose and trust me to do your will and not my own. I will forever praise your name for all that you've done for me and the lives that will be transformed as a result of you moving in my life.

My beautiful mother and amazing father for ALL you've done for Evan and me. Words can't express my love for you both. I'm so blessed to have you in my life with your wisdom and wit. I'm forever grateful. I think I have the best siblings money can buy, thank you Punkin, Vanita, Jonas, and Isiah for being supportive and never judging my circumstances. I remember calling you all first to tell you of the news before you heard about it on television. You immediately stepped in to assist me in any way I needed. We're a special bunch, but our love works for each other. Evan is so blessed to have amazing aunts and uncles in his life!

My baby boy Evan, you are truly my angel sent from The Father. He blessed me with you at the right time in my life. I'm sure when you are old enough to read this book; you'll have so many questions. You're the inspiration, and I want you to know that you are amazing and you can be anything you want to be in this life. Mommy will always want the best for you! Remember to forgive and love your neighbor in addition to following the Ten Commandments in life and our Father will continue to bless you.

I have the most amazing group of friends that I called my extended family. I'm truly blessed to call you all my sisters: Shameka, Tyana, Tanvia, Maria, Karli, Monet, Lolita, "The Sister Chain", and a host of others in the journey of writing the book. Those inspirational words, prayers, and conversations were the driving force behind the book. May The Father continue to bless your families, businesses, and everything you touch. It kept me pushing forward when times got a little rough for me on this journey. I love you all! A special acknowledgment goes to my Life Coach /Editor /and Friend Dr. Karen Ratliff. Girl. Thank you for being obedient to The Father's call and not being selfish with your gifts. It was through your guidance and expertise that allowed me to manifest my first book. I pray that The Father continue to bless my friends beyond your imaginations.

    Christian, thank you for encouraging and pushing me throughout this process of writing and keeping me in The Father's word. I appreciate your assistance with the creative process of the book cover and insight to the project itself. You are amazing, and I am truly thankful for you.

REFORM'D

Dedication

This book is dedicated to Yah (GOD)

REFORM'D

Chapter 1 – The Meeting

I met him in the month of December in 2005. We were at the Jewel Osco grocery store in a southwest suburb of Chicago, Illinois. I remember that day like it was yesterday because it was the moment that changed my life forever. The weather was cold, but it was sunny outside. I had been on my feet all day working and managing others as the Assistant Manager of the grocery store. I didn't like my job, but I didn't have a lot of options of places to work due to my lack of professional experience. However, I was content with the position because it allowed me to have a flexible schedule to attend college. I was able to complete school and maintain what I considered to be a high paying position. I was focused on being a straight "A" student and putting myself in a better financial position as an adult at the tender age of twenty.

REFORM'D

    I knew that I wanted something more in life than what I experienced growing up. It was through my observation of my surroundings and the lives of my colleagues and peers, who appeared to have more of a life's advantage over me, which caused me to recognize that something was missing in my life. Some individuals had an advantage over me as it related to professional experiences and life encounters. Knowledge of my peers' parents making six figures and living in a nice suburban area, I internalized that I would need to play catch up professionally, academically, and socially, in order to feel that I blended in with those around me. My classmates had cars and the luxury of driving to school daily. My reality was paying for public transportation from the south side of Chicago to Palos Hills. Because of the feeling of lack and sentiments of being left behind, I set personal goals to do better. My mindset was to put myself in a better position in order to achieve greatness. I wanted to be an established professional with good credit, a nice car, and a nice place to live. Those things were important because they were so foreign to me while growing up. There was no one in my immediate circle or family that possessed any of those things, nor was there anyone around who could show me how to obtain them. I needed mentors in my life to show me what being a grown-up really meant. All I had to look forward to was one day possibly renting my own apartment. There were some successful individuals in my family, but they didn't care to show me how they achieved success. I didn't have a professional mentor in my immediate reach. All I saw and experienced was the constant hustle around the idea of finding a job to simply survive and stay afloat. I believed that having the right man and career were my keys to success. I wanted other people to know that I was successful, despite my background and how I grew up. I often cared about what other's thought about me and their opinions about what I was doing and what I had. It was important for people to know that I could do great things and their opinion mattered in my mind. It was a stamp of approval. Similar to receiving the approval from your parents.

Growing up, I was talked about so much and picked on for the clothes and shoes I wore. I was called "dirty" and "ugly" for many years by my peers in the neighborhood and at school. That impacted my self-esteem for a very long time. I kept it inside and didn't tell anyone because I learned that speaking about it was a sign of weakness. Talking about my true, inner feelings were shunned on in my neighborhood. The *smell* of weakness and vulnerability could've gotten me picked on and targeted by kids in the neighborhood even more, and on a more consistent basis. Because I sought out to gain peer approval, it robbed me of my identity at a young age. I constantly adjusted in order to fit in with new trends, friends, and social activities. But it didn't help. Often times I felt defeated, anxious, and alone. These same feelings formed a competitive trigger that was wrapped around success.

My salary was very competitive while working at the grocery store. At the age of 21, I received a promotion pretty fast after high school, as a result of my hard work of course. The company presented opportunities for me to travel within the region and to work at different store branches. I took advantage of all of the opportunities. I was adamant about being a professional at all cost and desired to be promoted quickly. I felt like I could be successful in the banking industry and shortly began to pursue a career in that field. It was important for me to never see lack and poverty again. I wanted something different in life. I knew there was something brilliant inside of me and that the world needed to see it, whatever it was.

My upbringing was solid morally, but the crime infested environment wasn't ideal for my living situation. Experiencing success at such a young age was a motivator for me to keep moving in the direction of success – despite not having many mentors in my life. I desired to continue to seek professional prosperity so I wouldn't have to continue to live in the poverty-stricken neighborhood that I grew up in. I wanted to always move forward no matter what. I felt like it was all in my hands to make "being successful" happen. It was time for me to make *power boss moves* in my life and finally become successful.

The definition of success for me at that time consisted of getting all of the tangible things that I wanted. The material things that I gathered would determine my success. In actuality I had no direct control of my life, but I thought I did. Even at that age, I was aware that God controlled all things in my life. But, my curiosity and control took over and the adrenaline in my body was pumping at an all-time high - I loved it. I couldn't control it and I learned something about myself. I learned things quickly, I could be shown something once and remember it easily. I not only had the ability to pick up most skills quickly, I excelled at them, too. That's exactly what I did with the banking opportunity.

After sometime I was able to transition from the management side of the grocery store chain to begin working at the bank within the store. In my mind, the bank position gave me a chance to get the car that I wanted, establish more credit, get the apartment that I wanted, and generate an income that I could brag about a little bit. Not having a mentor created a disadvantage for me. It prevented me from understanding how to *connect the dots* and navigate through, not only my professional journey, but life in general. I felt like I couldn't go to my mother with my goals and what I would like to do because she wouldn't be able to help me.

My older sisters and brothers couldn't help either. They were doing their own thing and life for them at the time wasn't indicative of what I desired anyway. My brother was the first to get his college degree out of my mother's five children. My sister worked multiple jobs and life was good for her. So I silently followed the two of them from afar, hoping to mirror their lives in some way. I worked hard on my job as well to stay afloat, but I wanted more than simply just living. I wasn't satisfied and I wanted more for my future. No one had given me a blueprint of how to reach my ultimate goals. That was a major problem.

Don't get me wrong, there were some hard working individuals around me. My mother worked hard every day. She worked at a grocery store and eventually retired from a major hotel chain as a cook. My sisters and brothers worked hard as well. I felt for a very long time that we all worked to survive – even me.

I began to get the things I longed for, but it just wasn't enough. And soon I noticed my brothers and sisters hitting plateaus in their careers, they were not being promoted. They seemed to stay on the same level for so long. It didn't seem fair. No matter how hard we worked, we were still in the Woodlawn Gardens, where people seemed to have no hope or dreams whatsoever. I wanted a better life that consisted of nicer things. I wanted better than what I saw around me.

After some time, I started to grow tired of the day-to-day at the branch. There was nothing dynamic about the duties on the job and after a while it took a toll on me. I didn't feel satisfied or fulfilled by working there anymore. It was time for me to make some changes, but I didn't know which direction to go in because I had been in the financial sector for a long period of time. The days started to get very long and dreadful. I had no motivation in the morning to get ready for work. I became bored, even though I looked forward to seeing the people that I worked with at the job. They were full of energy and jokes on a daily basis, and it was never a dull moment with them around – but I wasn't fulfilled. The branch consisted of all women, both young and old. We were all African Americans, most with families, some with husbands, and all with responsibilities. They were like my little family outside of my real family. Working there wasn't the end for any of us, but we made the best out of it while we were there.

One of the workers was a comedian. I used to joke with her about how she missed her calling because she kept us laughing. She told a joke about every customer that walked through the door. It made our day go by fast and made the job bearable. In actuality, we hated the mundane day-to-day duties of the job and the customer service aspect of it because the people we serviced didn't treat us well.

During the time I was at the branch, I was in a relationship with my high school sweetheart for two years. It didn't work out with us because I was maturing much faster than he was, although he was about a year older. The more mature I became in age, the more mature I grew mentally. We grew apart and ended up breaking up as a result of his lack of maturity in my eyes. We remained friends when I ended things, but officially went our separate ways after some time. My profession and relationship dreams started to change, too. I felt that I needed to be connected to someone that could help me excel further in life. I didn't have a lot of money in savings, and my family did not have much money either. The opportunity for me to go into an account and withdraw money on my 18th birthday wasn't an option. I felt that because of my upbringing, I was at a disadvantage and I had to work harder than my peers in order for me to achieve the ultimate level of success. I once thought about how good it would feel to have a man in my life that could help me get a head start in life financially. I dreamt about moments where a financially secured man would be able to help me in every aspect of my life. I would have extra money in the bank and he would take care of my tuition bill, car note, and buy me clothes. The picture I had painted in my mind was everything I desired in a relationship. It was time for me to make it happen and make it my reality. After all, this is what so many young women in my neighborhood did, especially the cute ones. The girls used what they had physically, to get whatever they wanted. Usually, they received whatever they desired instantly. Initially, I spoke ill about that lifestyle and often stated that I would never date anyone who receives their money illegally. I was determined to attempt the route of success through the avenues of school and work, but success was taking entirely too long for me.

    The attractive women were able to get in relationships with men who provided for them monetarily. Those financial benefits allowed them to drive the cars they wanted, afford the designer clothes, and apartments of their own. Subconsciously, I wanted that too. I knew that way of life wasn't necessarily right, but I felt the experience would be worth the risk. I was willing and ready to take that risk, by any means necessary. So I did it. I desired to be with someone, anyone who would help me to the next level up. I figured that I didn't have much to lose – be careful what you ask for.

When he walked in the store and stood by the counter in the branch, I was instantly interested. He was tall and dark, well-dressed, and handsome. Another representative was in the process of taking care of him, so I stood back and just admired him from afar. I didn't want him to know that I was checking him out because I wanted him to notice me first. When I glanced over at him, he was looking down and finishing up his transaction with the other representative. There was something that caught my attention. Yes, he was handsome, but it was his confidence that caught my attention. I was attracted to tall confident men with a strong presence. He possessed that and more. I was very interested in him and wanted to find out who he was. After he completed his transaction with my co-worker, the conversation and gossip began about him among the group of women that I worked with. After about 15 minutes, I knew his name and where he stayed. The rep that took care of him was totally interested in him and entertained getting his number, but never acted on it.

 The next morning upon my arrival at work and a few hours into my day, I received a call from the front desk of the store. I thought that maybe it was a complaining customer whose transaction was entered incorrectly, or a potential customer who had questions on how to start a new account with us. It turned out to be the guy that we were gossiping about the day before. He called the store to get connected to me. I was totally thrown off guard and taken by surprise when he started to speak. My feelings were mixed because I thought to myself that maybe he had stalker tendencies, but on the same token I was impressed by the effort and that he chose to contact me.

REFORM'D

Being chosen was a big deal for me because I wasn't the popular girl in the neighborhood that the guys wanted. My body didn't develop until I became older and active in volleyball, cheerleading, and track. After high school, I got the attention from older men because of my outer appearance. I enjoyed the attention I received because it made me feel good. I felt that my office was full of ladies, but he selected me to pursue at the time, which was flattering.

Even though he caught my eye initially, I had some hesitant reactions towards him. In addition to the business he took care of with us, I noticed on the same day that he stopped at the coin machine to cash in some coins in exchange for dollars. I didn't equate a man being financially stable to cashing in coins to get cash from a generated receipt. That drew a concern for me and it didn't align with the plan that I mentally established to reap the benefits of what I thought would be a great life. So, I was a little apprehensive about the pursuit. It concerned me but it was really something about him that I wanted to entertain and see what he was about.

The phone call was very awkward. I was engaging in a conversation with a complete stranger who I've seen one time. There I was standing in my office speaking to him about our first date. I had no clue what his motive was or why he wanted to speak with me. How did he know I was at work that day? There were so many thoughts and questions going through my mind. After I said "hello", he immediately went into what he wanted from me. He told me that he wanted to take me out, and I had to give him my number. I laughed out of nerves and responded by saying, "excuse me!" He repeated himself and told me that he wanted to take me out. He then proceeded to ask about my schedule, where we should meet, and what we were going to do. I literally was in a state of shock while speaking with him.

After a very brief conversation, I gave him my number and agreed to meet him at the local movie theater for our first date. I thought to myself, *how can I refuse the offer?* In those follow up seconds I thought, *something had to be different, more exciting than my current situation. He may be worth the offer.* My life was so safe and predictable and it seemed that the people who were doing something completely different in life were doing better than me. I refused to go backwards. I felt like I had complete control of the outcome of my life. It was up to me to see and make the necessary changes that would allow me to learn, grow, and experience life on a level in which I've never experienced before. The level of success and happiness I wanted revolved around having money and the career I wanted. I wanted the fantasy, what I saw on television shows, the dream – I wanted it all. The feeling was powerful and overwhelming. How could I make this relationship work? What strategies could I use to make it happen? Am I good enough?

We met up at the theater like we discussed on the phone. It was a chilly afternoon in the city. My nerves were bad, but there was no turning back. I worked early and got off at 2pm that day. Before I left the branch I stopped in the restroom to freshen up. I didn't wear makeup, so *freshening up* consisted of lip-gloss and smoothing my hair down from any frizz that crept in from the day. My pants were above my ankles and I did not wear heels at all because I stayed on my feet all day. He and I didn't meet after the initial conversation, so I forgot how he looked.

At the time, I owned a brand new Chevy sedan that I was super proud of. It was burgundy with a nice sound system, which was all that mattered to me. I sat in the parking lot of the theater and waited for him to arrive as he instructed me to. I was edgy and anxious as it took him about 30 minutes to show up. I kept fixing my clothes and putting on the same cherry lip-gloss to make sure I looked good for him. I knew that he was somebody whom I needed to look the part for. He possessed the confidence and commanded the attention. His actions led me to believe that he was the boss of something or somebody. It made me feel a little insecure initially because I'd never been around a man who was that confident. After much anticipation, he pulled up in a gray Mercedes Benz 760 sedan with silver rims and a fresh car wash with a wax. My mouth dropped and I'm sure my heart skipped several beats. I said to myself, "Tinka you did it! This is what you deserve." I thought that I would not have any more mediocre relationship with another man. I believed that I finally met my equal and it was time to pursue him. I was very reluctant to get out of my vehicle because of my nerves were all over the place. I was intimidated because of the car that he drove and I equated what I saw to success and money. This was something I hadn't experienced yet in life, at least not much of it. He got out of the car dressed very nice and urban. He wore a bomber jacket, jeans, and a pair of Timberline boots. The way he walked over to my car with so much presence captivated me on all levels. I was anxious and eager to greet him with a hug. He wore assurance well and I wanted to be with him more because of it. He greeted me with a smile and a warm kiss. Before going into the theater, he asked me to follow him in my car to another store that was located in the same strip mall so he could purchase some items since we still had a good hour left to spare before the movie started.

There I was following behind his Mercedes Benz in my sedan. I felt so proud walking with him. I was conscious of how I walked and my posture. He made sure that I stayed on the inside of the sidewalk while we were walking. He was a gentleman. While shopping at that local clothing store, we realized it was time to get to the theater to see the movie. We were literally around the corner so we quickly went back to our cars and drove a few minutes to theater's parking lot. We parked our cars and headed to the theater holding hands. I was excited to be in his company. I couldn't read him at all because he didn't smile much or give expression. It was important for me to discover if he was serious about me or not. The movie that we saw was great and we concluded the night with a very long conversation while gazing into each other's eyes all night until it was time for me to go home. He told me that he had something to do as well so I didn't mind the *good bye* and *I'll see you soon* conversation that ended with a kiss. I felt special that night. I enjoyed his company and I knew right away that I wanted to be his woman and I got a strong feeling that he wanted to be my man. I was very honest with him at the beginning with the fact that I was in a relationship with another man but we were on bad terms at the time. He told me to tell my boyfriend to "beat it" and I did as he requested.

Chapter 2 – Baby and His Lady

As the days and weeks went by, he and I wouldn't talk much on the phone. He wasn't a talker, but he would show up at my job to pick me up for lunch and enjoy my company. He was nine years older than me. That wasn't unusual for me because I always dated men much older than I was. I felt like the guys my age didn't have anything to offer me. My experiences dating older men were very different compared to dating men my age. The conversations were of substance, dates were nicer, and I overall felt secured. I can attribute that to having aspirations in life to be married and most guys my age were in a different mind-set. I was very mature for my age and always looking for ways to evolve as an individual, there weren't many men that I encountered who could keep up with me. Or was I looking for someone who could fill that void that I had as a result of my father leaving the home and eventually divorcing my mother?

Was I looking for guidance in addition to a partner in my relationship? These were all contributing factors that intrigued me while dating older men. I noticed the dynamic of our relationship was very different than what I was used to. I was accustomed to talking on the phone for hours. It was not a problem for me to pop up at their home to visit and there were many dinner and lunch dates with them as well. This was not the reality in my new relationship. Getting in contact with him was always a struggle. He didn't pick up most of the time, and I usually wouldn't be able to speak with him until after 8:00pm. I knew that was odd, but I didn't want any push back from him. He didn't strike me as a man who entertained or liked drama.

It brought out some of my insecurities that led me to believe that there was another woman somewhere. Quite frankly, I thought that because he was much older than me and because I couldn't offer the relationship much that he had gotten bored with me and moved on to someone else. If that happened, my quest for a better life would end abruptly and that was something I refused to allow happen. I remember him telling me that I couldn't call him by his first name. I could only call him *Baby*.

At first, calling him *Baby* made me feel uncomfortable, but I did it and it grew on me. I felt like he was indirectly molding me into the woman he wanted in his life, and I was ready to comply with the plan. We had only known each other for a month and he placed some demands on our relationship very quickly that left me a little baffled. I couldn't go out much with my friends, I couldn't wear my hair in certain styles, and my clothes couldn't be too tight. Nevertheless, I went along with the flow of things and the requests that he made and immediately made the necessary changes to the way I responded to him. He was pleased at how fast I adjusted to being his woman. In hindsight, it was something that I wanted anyway and being with him made me feel different. I believed that we could one day get married and start a family. He was my definition of what I was looking for in a husband. He was simply someone who could take care of me. It was a feeling that I never felt before in any other relationship. What he had to offer in our relationship outweighed my concerns and insecurities that surfaced in that moment. Being submissive, attentive, and compliant were important factors to me. Being with him allowed me to set myself apart.

    I immediately noticed that he possessed some very dominate characteristics that I had only experienced with my father. Characteristics of being a protector, provider, and confidant. We went out to eat and he made sure that I was taken care of. I didn't have to order my dinner, even though it was awkward for me. I was a young woman who always took care of my own business. My father left the home when I was 10 and that negatively impacted my innocence, but I was a very dominate young woman as well. I knew what I wanted and where I was headed in life, at least that's what I thought. So Charlie ordering my food made me feel very safe. I felt like I didn't have to do much in our relationship and that he would take care of everything. I would be able to sit back and reap the benefits of truly being someone's woman, nothing more and nothing less. No longer did I want to be a mentor for men and show them how to do basic things in life, which is what I did with my ex boyfriends.

    I wanted a man who was, not only older than me in age, but also more experienced. Those things were important because of my need to have progression in my life. He put a demand on me by ensuring that my living conditions, vehicle, and wardrobe were all upscale. I never experienced that demand before and it intrigued me. I wanted the best of the best because I felt like I never had it and I deserved to experience the luxuries of life. I watched girls get it from observing them in the neighborhood and it was my turn. The man in my life had to have already been successful and goal driven before I dated him. No longer did I want to lead in my relationship. After all, isn't that the role of a man? I've always felt that my life would be extraordinary, but I didn't know how or when greatness would occur. I felt that things needed to happen on my terms because success was something that was in my reach and control. It was time for me to go out there and get it. No one would do the work for me and that very thought was enough for me to go after it all. The man, things, money, and lifestyle were literally knocking at my door and the time was now to receive it all.

I was brought up in a Christian household. I believed in God but didn't have a relationship with Him. I later learned that those are two completely different experiences. This was an area in which I was very lax in with the men I chose to be in my life. A man's credit, financial status, career, and business took precedence over his religious beliefs. These were things that I didn't necessarily grow up around. My dad made good money while serving in the military. He was able to take care of the household when things were good and when he wasn't strung out on drugs. My perception came from my assessment of what I saw in the neighborhood and television. There were great women in my life: my mother, grandmothers, and aunts, but their teachings were on different levels. Those levels included being ethical, having morals, cooking, and cleaning the house. Being equally yoked with someone was not a deal breaker for me. That's not an area that anyone sat down with me to discuss. No one shared with me the importance of being selective. I was okay with gambling with the idea of being with someone who had financial stability, but not a relationship with God. My ignorance to why made his financial status and his relationship with God two totally different focuses for me. If he had money, my emotions felt right about him. If he was attractive, that was enough for me to consider the relationship and move forward full throttle without hesitation. Even though I didn't have multiple sexual partners, nor did reckless things, I still wasn't living a holy lifestyle at that age.

While growing up, going to church was something that we had to do. Church services on Sundays were like a task for me to complete. I went through the motions of it, but not really getting anything out of it but a word on occasion. My occasional church attendance, when mandated by my mother, helped me establish a spiritual foundation that consisted of biblical scriptures and understanding God. I would later activate the very same spiritual foundation that would help me get through a tough life-changing shift.

    I was very serious about my relationship with Charlie and having a failed relationship was not an option, so I became submissive. It was like I hit the jackpot. He had everything that I dreamt of, money, cars, homes, and freedom - so it seemed. I wanted to prove that I was worthy of being his woman, by any means necessary. I was like a child who went out of her way to prove to a parent that she loved them. It was very important to me that he understood that I was willing to go out of my way to prove my love for him. My love had to be something completely different than what he'd experienced with anyone else, so he became my priority. Whatever he wanted from me, I had to make it happen, no matter what. I knew the odds were stacked against me because of my age and lack of experience. I called it love early on, but it was really lust. I had no clue what the word love truly meant as far as being in a relationship.

Because I didn't get a chance to see him often, I made our moments special when we did spend time together. I treated him as if he was my husband. I did things that naturally came to mind from my memories being a child and watching my mother. I cooked, cleaned, and took care of him whenever he was around me. I didn't have my own apartment yet because I couldn't afford to at 21, but he had a condo up north near Montrose in Chicago. I wasn't over regularly but the times that Charlie summoned me to his place, I spent the night over with him to simply engage in sex with him. I wanted him to love me at all cost. That was my attitude towards him. My mother never questioned those times that I did not come home. The nights of driving down Lake Shore Drive listening to Jamie Fox's *Unpredictable* album helped me get through the 30 minute drive from Cottage Grove to the Montrose exit via Lake Shore Drive. Driving through the roughest parts of Chicago through downtown of the city to a different world brought a smile on my face. A sigh of relief, and success that most aren't privy to experience, overtook me in those moments of seeing him. I thought to myself, *this is where it will begin*. My new life experiences will begin here, with him, and it will never be the same. Those trips continued a minimum of twice per week.

As the relationship progressed, deep down I knew there was something wrong. As we pillow talked and he exposed me to who he really was, questions started to formulate in my mind that I was afraid to ask.

Seeing him switch cars like I changed clothes on a daily basis concerned me. The massive amounts of cash on hand shocked me because I never experienced anything remotely close to it before, so it didn't seem normal. The telephone numbers of other women, multiple phones, and women's clothing that I found in random places around his apartment, were all signs that he wasn't being honest about whom he was. He told me that he made an honest living being a successful real estate investor and traded currency on his own time, but something just didn't add up for me. I witnessed him buying and trading commodities one evening in his apartment. He would stay up late at night on the computer and on the phones with a broker having conversations about trades and the amount of money that needed to be invested. The amount of the checks that were coming in from trading didn't match his purchases. The brand new Mercedes Benz 760 was one of the many cars that he owned. The expensive jewelry and the abundance of clothes and shoes didn't add up to the $3,000 check that I saw him make from trading. He used that money to invest back in the market to trade commodities again.

The more time that we spent together, the more my perspective started to change about what he did for a living. I didn't want to ask many questions either. I didn't know and I really didn't want to know the details of what he was doing because I was actually excited about the opportunity of finally being with a man who could take care of me no matter what. My days of figuring everything out on my own were over. This was the opportunity that I dreamt about as a young girl. Seeing the *it girls* in the neighborhood date the handsome men and getting whatever they wanted intrigued me, and I wanted to be a part of the experience. It didn't make it right but I knew that I couldn't pass on the opportunity. Therefore, I proceeded with caution in every action, reaction, and response when it came to him. Although he never said it to me, I felt like I couldn't question him because I would run the risk of making him angry. But it was eating at me about the unknown of the truth of his lifestyle. He was the type of man that would've been able to finesse his way out of a jam easily, so asking questions about things that concerned me would not have been successful. I felt like I could be replaced at any moment so I treaded lightly with a lot of things pertaining to him to avoid conflict and a potential break up.

    At moments I felt an urge to ask questions about why he stayed out so late, the multiple phone calls received, and inconsistent communication. At that point, I was in too deep. I verbally gave him my commitment that we were in a relationship and I was willing to be committed no matter what. I felt obligated to show him that what I stated was true because I wanted to be different. I didn't want to be seen as the average 21 year old that he decided to date. I felt obligated to show him my loyalty from that point on. I knew that I had his buy-in and refused to disturb the rapport that we built between us. I didn't think he was in love with me at the time but I was in love with him. If he was, he had a weird way of showing it. His responses to me and lack of verbal confirmation led me to believe that he was very interested but not in love the way I wanted him to be.

As time progressed, I started to reap the benefits of being his woman. He helped me get my first apartment and made sure that it was fully furnished. He was adamant about making sure that my lifestyle matched his so he took care of every bill to furnish my first apartment. We went to a furniture store in a south suburb to shop and he paid for everything cash. I was only 22 at the time and had never done anything close to shopping without a limit. I felt like Julia Roberts from the movie *Pretty Woman*. I literally pointed and got every item that I needed. Location was very important to him when I selected a place, so he made it a priority to be a part of the decision on where I moved. He told me that it was important where he would lay his head. I wondered why because it wasn't a big deal for me. He was really particular and anal about things that I wasn't conscious of. I didn't put myself in dangerous situation and I was a bit naive of the difference between certain areas of the city, but he was well-versed. I had to grow up very quickly in our relationship. My potential impressed him the most because I was very impressionable and coachable. He guided me with much ease and I know that's where an abundance of his patience came from. He knew exactly what he wanted to mold me into. The sedan that I was proud and excited to buy and drive no longer did it for him. He told me that his woman couldn't drive an ordinary car, so he immediately gave me the keys to his Range Rover Silver Sport truck until he was able to purchase me a two door black Benz Coupe. I was so happy and ecstatic about the opportunity because I never owned a luxury vehicle and I felt that I had "made it." I drove through my neighborhood so the people that I grew up with could see me. As children, we were talked about and made fun of for not having the best wardrobe and shoes. Well, this was an opportunity for me to rub it in without even using my words to do so. I let them *see* the success I created for myself. Being able to drive those high quality vehicles boosted my self-esteem to the point of no return. I thought to myself that my plan had finally manifested. *Or did it?* Was it a manifestation or a life detour? This was the life that I only dreamt about. A man found me. He was well established and goal oriented. He seemed to be head over heels for me and since he was nine years older than me, there was still some growing that I needed to do as well.

I really wasn't settled in my career, I had great credit, but no property or other assets to show for it. I still needed to figure some things out, but I knew that he saw the potential in me and that was probably the reason why he made me a priority in life and began take our relationship more seriously. He groomed me from the inside out and it showed in my appearance and demeanor. I never thought that I would be able to break the strongholds of my upbringing in poverty. I was in my late twenties when I came to the realization that I had a stronghold. I was okay with the familiar feeling and being complacent and going without, but I didn't like the feeling of being controlled by these feelings. I forced myself to get up and be productive.

The mental strain of not knowing how to break the cycle was frustrating. The internal limitations of me feeling inferior because I feared the unknown became my reality. It was happening for me and happening fast. There was no turning back. Nothing was going to make me miss the life changing opportunity. I knew that my world was going to be different - but would it be better forever?

In addition to the cars that I had access to, he made sure that I wore the best clothes, shoes, and jewelry. Because of his reputation, I had to look like I belonged to him no matter what. I didn't know why it was so important for me to always be in name brand attire for the sake of his reputation, but I was. He would always say that he had "street credibility." I was totally out of the loop on what that meant. I didn't pay it any attention or second-guessed that he wanted the best for me as his woman. Ultimately, I enjoyed every bit of the perks that came my way. No other man had ever showed me that much attention. However, Charlie didn't fill my emotional bank compared to the men in my past relationships, but whatever I wanted in regards to clothes, money, and shoes, I got it from him. It was very familiar to me because it's the way that my father treated me when he was in the home. Before leaving for two weeks with the National Guard, he bought me whatever I wanted and took me to the most amazing venues in downtown Chicago. Those things stopped once he started using drugs to the point of no return.

Charlie also made me feel special and important. He could do no wrong in my eyes. I ignored so many things early on that would've been red flags had it been anyone else. I put the pieces together as far as what he did for a living. I drew my conclusions from very close observation of his demeanor, which included, the patterns in which he was in and out the house, and the different stories that he told me about how he would generate money.

I knew that it was a lifestyle that my family would not be pleased of. His lifestyle was his way of living that I knew about through casual gossip with my friends in the neighborhood. A lifestyle that included quick opportunities to get what was desired without considering the risks and how it would negatively impact a family. His lifestyle, as I knew would only end in two ways, death or incarceration.

Chapter 3 - Lost Girl

I got to the point where I lost my identity. Inwardly, my insecurities where taking over. I started to feel that I was not good enough and didn't have much to offer the relationship anymore. Often times I didn't feel pretty enough to be with him. I felt that because he was so financially successful, he could go out and find another woman to replace me at any moment. I convinced myself that it was important for me to obey and be compliant in the relationship. I started giving myself accolades for my life changing drastically at an early age. I felt like I had to put in the work for a different outcome, different from what I experienced in my past. I always sought jobs that would add an increase to my salary. It was important for me to be in different networking circles, so I would go out on occasion to meet new people. That was in conjunction with me doing the necessary work for the betterment of my life.

Though I was a bit insecure, ultimately I felt safe with Charlie and at the age of 22, I believed that I made it to the top. I envisioned and daydreamt about such things happening to me. Through it all, there was something knocking at my spirit. A knocking of spiritual conviction that I often times ignored. It was a familiar feeling, one that I've felt at a young age when my grandmother played one of her pastor's sermons on television and the word resonated in my spirit. I wasn't willing to explore what was behind that knock at my spirit or find a church home to bridge the gap. I had a grip on everything around me. Nothing needed to be done on my end because I was doing everything right and things seemed to be falling in place.

However, spiritually I knew I did things that weren't right. The money was coming in too fast,

Charlie's availability was sometimes unpredictable, and I still had no clear answer on what he did for a living. I was at risk of losing everything that was created in my world because of the pulsation that occurred quite often in my soul. I was in so deep that I physically couldn't hide it at times. My moments of deep thought and moral conviction tried to get the best of me. I wouldn't surrender nor give in. I remained confident that all would be well in due time.

While dating him, I didn't know at that moment, but God had granted me with the gift of discernment. I didn't have proof, but I didn't need it in order to know that what he sold to me, as far as his occupation, wasn't accurate. The more time we spent together the more we were able to get to know one another on a personal level. I met his mother and his twin brother who he didn't spend a lot of time with. His younger brother was locked up, so I didn't get a chance to meet him. I noticed a pattern in his family. Everyone had been to jail at some point and for long periods of time. Prior to us meeting, he had been in the federal prison for over a decade. That wasn't information that he voluntarily gave me. I did a brief background check on him while at school on break one day between classes. I remember looking at the computer and reading the details of his case in shock at what I read. He had been in jail for over a decade for a drug case that had some connection with some dangerous people in the early 90's. So many questions started to form in my head about him and whether or not the relationship was for me. It alarmed me but I didn't interrogate him about it. I felt like it was his past and he served his time, so I should let it go and not make a big deal about it. In that moment I knew that I couldn't take him home to meet my mom and definitely not my brothers. I was ashamed and embarrassed because of who he was so I hid him from my family for a very long time. I didn't want to deal with the backlash or judgment due to his background or his past decisions. While hiding him from my family, I hid myself from them as well. My relationships with my mother and brother diminished when they found out about my new relationship. I was an introvert who was very private, so I didn't share a lot of things going on in my life. I was a very shy person and it was hard for me to let people in, which is not an excuse to not tell my family about my new relationship. My brother was upset at me because I didn't formally introduce him to my boyfriend, and as my big brother he wanted to meet the person that I was dating. To be honest, I hadn't done that with any of the men I dated. My sisters didn't do it with their boyfriends, so I didn't think it would be a big deal when I followed their lead. My dad wasn't around during those tender times to teach me how to properly date, so I did it my way. I was content with the world I created for myself. All seemed to be well, but deep down inside, I knew that the choices I made would eventually catch up with me. I knew better morally, but my lifestyle had turned into lust and addiction to a man, and I enjoyed it. I relished in the adrenaline rush knowing that every day would be different with the dynamics of our relationship because he lived on the edge. He surprised me with dinners, trips on occasion, and he bought me whatever I wanted at any time.

Our lifestyles were completely opposite in what we believed in, our spiritual views, and lifestyles. They say opposites attract, and I believed that to be true with us. We didn't have much in common at all, especially with the nine-year age gap between us. It was clear that he knew more, experienced life, and could offer solutions better than I could. I trusted him without hesitation. If I needed a bill paid, advice, or protection, he was able to assist without hesitation. As a result, his rules had to be followed. I followed his lead in every situation. Paying attention to detail or the lack thereof was a big deal for him. He would get mad and stop speaking to me for days if I made a mistake on a task. He was very adamant about me following his lead as well. If I wasn't at his house when he wanted me to, he had a problem with that. If I wore weave to change my hairstyle and look, he demanded that I take it out.

    One day, he was in the hospital recovering from a critical motorcycle accident from hitting a tree. He paid for me to go to Miami with one of my best friends that same weekend. I decided to put some extensions in my hair and that was the first thing that he saw while visiting him before I caught my flight. He was angry and that turned into a verbal chastising and I didn't respond or defend myself. I was an adult being controlled by someone who I was in a relationship with, but felt as if he was my parent. I knew it was wrong, but I was in the most submissive state that I had ever been in before. No man in my life before Charlie, had ever brought me to my most submissive state. I turned the man in my life into my God. No longer was I praying and seeking the Lord. I was too busy doing everything necessary to gratify Charlie in every way: physically, mentally, and spiritually, so I thought. Those were his expectations for me in our relationship and it was important that I delivered.

    He became my priority and everything he wanted me to do took precedence over my family, education, and friends. The consequences of making the decision not to put him first were critical, and he made sure that I felt his disappointment when I didn't follow his rules. There were times that he wouldn't como to my apartment on purpose to spend time with me, as I desired. He knew that was something that would anger me. The mental struggles behind it drove me crazy. I wasn't sure if it was other women in the picture, which brought in insecurities that I had to deal with. I remember checking his cell phone one night just to see random pictures and text messages from other women that I assumed he was seeing. In addition, there was another cell phone that he kept from me.

    I began to fear him. Fear was something that I had when I thought about bringing the information to his attention regarding what I found in his phone, including other women numbers. I allowed my insecurities to grow as a result and dealt with it internally. It took me a while to do it, but I finally had the conversation with him about the random telephone calls, unknown phone numbers, pictures, and videos of other women. I wasn't ready for his reaction regarding the information that I discovered. He never admitted to my allegations of the things that I saw in his phone. Instead he threatened to leave the relationship and walked out of my apartment. He knew what to say and how to react to make me stay. My self-esteem was broken and I had become a bit timid and disconnected from my spirit. I felt soulless and not confident in my own skin because I wanted to please him and be the woman that he wanted me to be. It didn't feel right but I wanted him, so my feelings didn't matter. I just went with the flow of things.

The spirit of desperation and fear arose in my body like lava from a volcano. I went into desperation mode and called him about 20 times back to back for a few hours pleading and begging that he stay with me. I apologized numerous times in hopes that he would forgive me for going through his phones. But that didn't work. The times that I called him, he didn't pick up the phone for me and refused to spend a night at my place. When he was angry, he isolated himself from me entirely. I felt like he could replace me at any giving moment without hesitation. I didn't feel valued in those moments to be in his life. I remember sitting in the middle of my living room floor weeping until my head started hurting with intensity. I knew that it was over between us and there was no turning back. The only way for me to get his attention was to do something extreme and hurt myself physically. I could hear a voice in my head saying, "Go ahead and do it. This will get his attention and you will get him back because he will feel sorry for you and forced to stay. The harm will make him feel bad about the decision that he made to leave you."

As a result, I grabbed a steak knife from my kitchen drawer and sliced my left arm five times. There was no pain. I was numb from the reality of what I was doing. All I could think about was the fact that there was no turning back and had to carry out the physical harm that I inflicted upon myself in order to get that man back in my presence. I knew the life that I became accustomed to would be over without him. He was not replaceable. I did not know anyone who had such an impact on my life. Because of Charlie, my life changed drastically from rags to riches, so I thought.

I convinced him enough in the conversation for him to come back to my place. I would never forget him telling me something along the lines of, "that's it?!" when he got to my apartment. He basically said that what I had done to myself wasn't severe enough and I had made it seemed so bad over the phone. When things settled between us, he eventually started to put his clothes back in my closet and came around more. My emotions confused me to the point that I lost my identity. I didn't know who "Tinka" was because he had made me alter myself in so many of my ways. I dressed different for him. I wanted to wear gym shoes, jeans, and cute shirts. He demanded that I wore high heels and dresses. I couldn't wear hair extensions, which I did on occasion because it was fun to me. My behavior was that of a high-class girlfriend and that was not my true identity.

My true personality was that of a shy, young woman still breaking into adulthood and trying to find herself through the dynamic waves of life. In my mind, I knew that's who I was supposed to be. Instead, I was insecure and confused, yet still in a submissive state to him. It was important that he always knew that my world revolved around his because he meant the world to me. He never had to verbally tell me to think or have those feelings. He demanded it with a pierced look and his dominate demeanor. He didn't repeat himself at all. He hated that so I was very careful when it came to my actions and reactions to him. I listened attentively every time he spoke.

REFORM'D

My life had no value in that moment and I prepared to suffer as a result of the decision I made to harm myself. I felt hopeless, embarrassed, and disconnected from my life. I never felt so empty and dark in my life. I had no control of the feeling because it was so overwhelming. I wanted his attention. He was the best thing that happened to me. I had no outlet either. My family wouldn't understand. My best friend hated him and I had to save face for everyone else because they thought that my life was going so well. That incident would set the tone of our relationship. He knew that he had won and gained control over me. It was in fear of losing him and he was well aware of it. The fear and insecurities that transpired as a result of that led into alcohol use to numb the pain. On nights that I was alone, I sat in the middle of my floor and drank until I couldn't drink anymore. The drinking helped mask the pain and anxiety. The feeling of shame and guilt settled and as a result, my emotions were all over the place mainly because of whom I was turning into. I needed something to allow my mind to stop racing and overthinking the dynamics of the relationship. The infidelity and distrust that I refused to speak about forced me to suffer internally and silently. I felt like I wasn't good enough for him because of the person that I thought he was and my background didn't seem to compliment his. I overcompensated with the attention and nurturing that I gave him. I wanted to make sure that my care for him stood out. Therefore, I consistently cooked, cleaned, went to the cleaners, and was sexually active with him.

    He didn't stay home for long periods of time. I was disappointed about that. I wasn't with a man who valued spending time with me. Spending a lot of time with him was very important because I truly believed that helped to build a strong relationship that eventually would turn into a serious one.

Marriage was the ultimate goal in my mind for our relationship. Inside I knew that he wasn't the one and that what we had was a phase in my life. There was something bigger and greater out there for me, but I didn't allow it to become my reality. Instead, I wanted to make him love me and wanted him to be my husband one day. I knew that if I could show him how hard I could love, he would follow suit. He hinted to the fact that we would eventually get married as we progressed in our relationship one day but on his terms. He didn't say it but it was the tone he set in the relationship. This came from a man that forced me to tell him that I loved him. He corrected me when I didn't tell him that I loved him. For a long time I felt obligated to agree with him to avoid any confrontation. I feared the unknown with him so I wanted to make everything right for the sake of the relationship. In return, he took care of me financially and made sure I looked the way that he expected me to.

    I only met one of his friends who later passed away. It was an interesting situation to me. His friend spent a decade in prison for murder. Upon his release he decided to live life the right way and became a productive citizen in society. He secured a job and cut hair part time at a barbershop located on the Southside of Chicago. His past caught up with him one night at his home. A group of men broke into his place, while he slept and killed him in his home in front of his children and fiancée. They survived a jump from the 3rd floor apartment front room window. Charlie later told me that it was rumored to be the family of the person he murdered a decade ago had come back seeking revenge for the murder of their family member.

REFORM'D

After hearing his account of the story, I instantly knew that I was in a relationship with a dangerous man. The thought of it made me feel very uneasy about being with him, but I quickly got over it. I never expressed my feelings to him as a result of learning about what happened to one of his best friends. This was someone who he had grown up with and the only person that he trusted to meet me. He didn't have many friends that I knew about. I learned of another one of his best friends that, too, was killed because of the life style that he chose to live. This guy was well known in the Roseland community. I learned from a close friend, while looking at his obituary one day, that he was well known for robbing high-ranking drug dealers from different neighborhoods in the city. People would pay him to carry out certain vicious acts against people. After hearing that information, I immediately called him with the information that I got from my friend.

I was driving a truck that belonged to a man who was known to rob and kill people in the city of Chicago. Of course he defended his friend and assured me that I shouldn't be upset or nervous about the information that I received. He knew that all it took was a conversation to calm me down. I trusted his every word no matter if it was good or bad. We went through so much in our relationship that he was able to navigate us through so his credibility was good with me.

Subconsciously, I knew that he was involved in much more than he chose to reveal. I didn't have concrete proof but there were so many clues that led me to believe that it was indeed more to his lifestyle that I could ever fathom. I thought about leaving on so many occasions but I didn't have the confidence to leave. The dependency that was created in the relationship gave him the advantage to control my thoughts, feelings, and decisions. I voluntarily gave him the right to control my behaviors, thoughts, and feelings while we were together. I gave him all of my energy and always included him in my decisions no matter what. In my mind I belonged to him. My spirit didn't want to settle but my flesh couldn't resist.

Chapter 4 – I Was Locked Up, Too

After five years of being in the relationship, I became well aware of whom he was. I decided to stay with him despite the bad that I saw over time. In my mind, good always wins no matter what, so I knew things would overturn as a result of how I treated him. I continued to cater to his every need whenever he needed and wanted me to. There were some good and bad times like any other relationship I had been in. Unfortunately, there were more bad moments than good ones. I experienced everything including cheating, lying, and manipulation. I had gotten to the point where I felt like I had no other choice but to take it, deal with it, and hope for the best. Just when I thought the momentum of our relationship was going great, a sudden shift happened that brought shock to my world. The man that brought so much to my world was pulled over for a routine traffic stop and taken into custody because of some "unresolved issues" that happened in his past. The ironic thing about it was I didn't find out about the situation until a couple of days after it happened. I was immuned to him not being around a lot. It was the routine of the relationship. I didn't know exactly what he was doing those nights that I didn't see him or when I would call him and get no answer. My friend took me to a seafood restaurant and out of the blue, I got a phone call from his mother explaining to me what happened to him. Before I got that call from her, I was very quiet and distant because I just didn't know what was going on with him and there was no way for me to find out either. My insecurities kicked in and I was confused as to why I wasn't the primary point of contact. I immediately went into panic mode. There were so many thoughts going through my mind, and I kept asking myself *what's next? What are you going to do?* I was certain that my life would change because he was in jail and I didn't have any details as to when they would release him.

He was housed at the Cook County Correctional Center located on the Southside of the City. After a few days of not knowing what was happening with him, he called to let me know that he was okay and everything with his case and charges would be fine. I believed him and that conversation eased my anxiety entirely. He was locked up for just the weekend and he had the money to get bonded out which was about $20K.

His mother took care of the transaction at the courthouse. I stopped all activities that weekend. I did not party with my friends or socialize. My man was in jail and I felt my life had come to a sudden halt because he was such a huge part of my existence, so I thought. I didn't pick him up from the correctional facility (I'm not sure who did because I had to work late that day). I was excited to see him, and I thought that his past was over and life would go back to normal. I later found out that a new criminal charge was brought up because of a situation that happened in his past. He didn't get into many details and assured me that everything would be fine and not to worry. I believed him. As a result of him being locked up, we spent more time together. He even decided to take me out to dinner more. The relationship appeared to take on a new perspective and I was happy with it. However, he continued to stay out late at night and I suddenly found myself back into the old routine. It just didn't bother me anymore. He used to tell me that he had to take care of business in the streets, meaning in his neighborhood, which require his immediate attention. I got tired of arguing with him about how he needed to spend more time with me. I was at a point where I had to take what I could get out of him when it came to our relationship. I asked myself why it was so hard for him to adjust to a healthy relationship. I felt like he didn't know how to be a loyal, committed family man and that's what I desired of the man in my life.

As time went by I became complacent with the way things were and I constantly told myself that clearly I was his number one since he took care of my needs. Besides, I met his family and he trusted me to handle important things in his life. In my mind that was enough. It comforted my insecurities on that level, but on other levels I still had doubts. I saw so many inconsistencies with what he told me versus the reality of how he made money to support us. He was involved in some more illegal things that I later found out about. It wasn't voluntary information that I received directly from him either. I learned of those things just by observing him a lot and listening to his conversations. I always knew that things didn't add up, but I went along with it all for the sake of keeping our relationship. I was five years in at this point. I wasn't going to allow that time to go to waste. I felt like if I could hold on a little longer, he would just somehow change his ways and live his life right with me by his side. That wasn't the reality of the situation. His mindset was different. There were no options to consider. His way was the only option and there were no negotiations and conversation of what should or shouldn't be. It didn't matter if the topic involved an outfit that I wanted to wear, he had to be considered in that decision-making process as well. I stayed, despite of how it looked in terms of him going to jail and not living up to my expectations of what his part should be in the relationship. But on the other side of staying it made me feel powerless. I really didn't have much of a choice but to comply with everything. The unknown was scarier than staying – I decided to take my chances. He set the tone in the relationship. He was in charge and the boss of me. We often had conversations where he told me that I belonged to him and I needed to ask his permission for everything that I was involved in and wanted to do. I lacked confidence in knowing that if he wasn't the person that God wanted me to be with. I'm sure God had someone better in store for me, but I wasn't ready to see it that way. Those very same insecurities left me in a vulnerable state to please him no matter what. The most important thing I had in mind was to do whatever it took to please him. In return, he was happy with my behavior and for that I was pleased to do whatever it took to keep him in a good place. The farthest thing from my mind was the likelihood that he may go back to jail and spend more time away. There was no way he would allow that to happen to us.

On a nice evening in Chicago one weekend day, he decided to take a trip to California to meet with some *business partners* about some real estate ventures that he was interested in. I was suspicious about why he would take so many weekend trips there, but I didn't question it. I booked the flights for him even though he never wanted me on those trips with him for reasons unknown.

The trips were very quick as well. Leaving on a Friday would mean that he would return by Sunday or Monday the following week. I checked the status of the flight to make sure he took off and landed safely, that's how intense my anxiety was because I was frightened that he would get locked up. During his last trip there, I dropped him off at the airport and kissed him good-bye. It was something about that visit that made me feel uneasy and not confident about his departure. I drove home in silence and deep thought. There were many things going through my head regarding what was really happening in San Diego. Was it another woman?

Did he catch up with some people from his past? I was confused and afraid because I didn't know what to believe and reluctant to ask questions. We communicated the entire weekend. He called to let me know that he had made it to the hotel room and everything was good. He was due to come back on that following Monday after being gone since Friday. I got up Monday morning and did my regular routine. At this point, I worked at an online school in the Admissions department in downtown Chicago. I decided to leave the bank because he said that I wasn't making enough money at the bank and I needed a better salary in order to be approved for a home loan. He said that I should bring home no less than $1,000 every two weeks and the fact that I wasn't meant that I was settling. I was ecstatic when the job called me back with a salary offer of $38,000. The significant change in income made me feel like I accomplished a great feat. I never thought that I would be able to make that amount of money. I gave him credit for pushing me to find something else. He didn't mind verbally telling me that he played a huge part with helping me reach that milestone either.

    I remember being a frequent rider on the CTA train and used the bus system to commute back and forth to work. He was too busy during the day to pick me up and drop me off back home. When I boarded the train and sat down, I immediately reached out to him in high hopes that he would pick up and let me know that everything was good on his end, but I didn't get an answer. Not getting an answer was normal on his trips to California so I wasn't alarmed initially. I kept reaching out to him throughout the day and asked him to call me to make sure that he was okay. I received nothing in return. I started to get worried. I couldn't get any work done at the office and I started to pace the floor of the office thinking hard while strategizing my next move to get in contact with him. My last option was to get online and search San Diego's county jail database to see if he was in jail. I was reluctant because I knew that more than likely he was indeed incarcerated. Before I went online to search his name, I checked with the airline that he was due to come back on. The customer service representative confirmed that he was not on the flight back to Chicago from San Diego.

That was confirmation for me in making the conclusion that he was locked up. As I went online through Google to search San Diego's prison facilities, I had to brace myself for the outcome of my search. I was scared and had so much anxiety at the time. I didn't want to fathom the idea of him being back in jail after it seemed like he just got home from the first round of his stay at Cook County. As I typed in his name and pressed enter, the computer hesitated for a minute before loading the results. During that minute that seemed like an eternity to me, my thoughts and feelings were clouded. Finally, the results were in and my nightmare had become a reality again. He was back in jail, but this time in a different state and jurisdiction. The description of the charges was not online. In that moment all I could do was react and cry on my friend's shoulder, she also worked with me at the time. I just didn't understand how this could happen to me again. I tormented myself internally with questions as if it was my fault that he was locked up. I thought there was something that I could've done differently on my part. It was his actions that put him there yet I took accountability for it. For the rest of the day, I couldn't focus on my job and decided to leave work for the day and went straight home. I had no way of communicating with him for a few weeks. He finally reached out first through mail and then he was able to call me from San Diego's County jail. I was so happy to finally speak with him because I wanted to know exactly what took place and how he allowed himself to be back behind bars, yet again. He didn't give me a lot of information about what was going on, but I was able to piece it together as time progressed. Because he still had a case pending in Chicago, the Federal government had a hold on his immediate release because of the charges that were brought against him in California. There wasn't a bond necessary because the case was considered a misdemeanor in the State of California and it was settled very quickly. At the conclusion of the case, the U.S. Marshalls picked him up for a transfer back to Chicago. The transport process took a few days to happen. During that time, I decided to make sure that everything was prepared. I knew that he would need money on his books and my phone account needed to be readily available for him to call me when he could. I had the means to do it with the money that I made on my job and I didn't have many bills that I needed to take care of. The extra money was available for me to help out in whatever way I could. I felt like it was my duty to show him that I could take on the responsibility of making sure that he had whatever he needed while incarcerated. It was important that I made him proud of me and show him that I was capable of being his future wife. I was very proactive with what he needed. I made sure that money was available for commissary and I wanted him to see that I was able to hold it together so that I could support him mentally. It took him a week to get processed and assigned housing for his time at the Federal Metropolitan Correctional Center. The MCC facility was a temporary housing facility due to his federal probation violation. It was the first opportunity that I would be able to see him in a month. I was able to see him face-to-face where I would have every opportunity to ask questions and get more information about what the future held for his case.

The day finally came for us to see each other. He mailed a visitation form for me to fill out in order for the federal officers to clear my background for visitation. I sent it back the same day, and I was cleared and ready to see him that next week. The MCC facility was located in downtown Chicago, the heart of the city. The inmates had a 360 view of the city and a rooftop terrace at their disposal to use during recreational time daily. His visitation days were on Wednesdays all day and Saturday mornings. The weekday visitation was at a perfect time as I would be able to leave work and get to him in 15 minutes.

The first visit was exciting because I hadn't seen him in a month since dropping him off at the airport to head to San Diego. I had mixed feelings of excitement, nervous, and anger.

REFORM'D

Nonetheless, I wanted to make sure that I looked great, so I wore jeans and a nice tight top that showed my breast and the jeans accentuated my thighs. The Metropolitan Correctional Center officers were very strict on attire, so I had to be very careful to make sure that my clothes weren't too tight, otherwise they would deny my visit for the day. I parked my royal blue Cadillac truck in the parking lot next to the prison. The building was adjacent to the parking lot. I took my purse and the extra money to pay for food during the visit as stated in the handbook that I read on their website. As I walked in the door and looked around me, the room was filled with majority women and children waiting to see their love ones who were incarcerated. The guards instructed me to fill out a form that they compared to their database to determine if I was on the approved guest list for him. After everything checked out, the guard gave me a key that I used to gain entry to a locker that was assigned to me to house my things for the rest of the evening. There was nothing allowed upstairs in the visiting room with the inmates. The risk of visitors bringing things in for the inmates was high. The prison was cold and it gave me a feeling of uneasiness. The staff were rude and uptight. I guess that is to be expected when you're managing "dangerous" people. I quickly put my things away and kept my money, lip gloss, and locker key with me. I placed it all in a small plastic sandwich bag that was on the list of approved things to take with me. The restroom was next door to the lockers, so I headed there afterwards to make sure that my hair, clothes, and of course lip-gloss looked great. I wanted to look good for him and that was expected of me anyway in the relationship, so I had to look the part. Nothing changed because he was in jail. The same rules applied so it was important for me to represent him well.

The prison visits were really starting to take a toll on me and at times it was depressing. I never communicated my feelings to him because I knew that I could handle it. He wasn't aware that while he was gone, I didn't go to the hairdresser every week, and I had no interest in keeping myself up because he was not around. Because I suffered internally, I had no ambition to do anything for myself. I just worked to occupy my time and watched television when I was home. I got my motivation to get myself together once I knew for sure that he was back in Chicago and that I had an opportunity to see him, hug him, and converse with him about the issues that had abruptly taken place in our lives.

The time came and my group was next to go up to see our loved ones. When the guard called my name, I was instructed to get in a single file line. The guard then gave me a gray bin to place all of my belongings in order to pass the security check, similar to what I've seen at the airport. The security check machine was very sensitive causing me to go back and forth several times in order to be cleared. I was on the last attempt before my visit would be denied. It turned out to be the wire in my bra that kept triggering the machine to go off. Nevertheless, I passed the security check-point and was ready to head upstairs. The guard then read a disclosure about the visit pertaining to illegal drugs being brought to inmates, sexual activity in the visiting room, and the consequences if the rules were broken. At that point, my anxiety had risen several levels because I was very excited to see him, but the process was taking too long for me. I just couldn't sit still. Between the guards who hated their jobs and kids crying, an hour had already past. I was about ready to open the gate myself and head up on the elevator to the 23rd floor to the visitation room.

Finally, it was time, the gate opened and the group proceeded to the holding area before the elevators. Three guards watched us closely. The two who accompanied us upstairs and the one that stood silently in the watch-tower waiting for his guards to give him the "all clear" signal. The temperature in the building got colder as we prepared to enter the elevator. There were majority African American and Hispanic women on the elevator with their children. I saw one Caucasian family, maybe twice, during my journey going back and forth to the facility. As the elevator door closed and we headed to the 23rd floor, several thoughts crossed my mind. I didn't understand why women were bringing their sons and daughters to a prison. I told myself I would never allow my child to see anything remotely close to a prison under any circumstances. I didn't have any children at the time so it was easy for me to say that without being in their shoes. I can only imagine what they had to deal with being single mothers in the household while the father completes a prison term for a crime. It was something that I promised myself that would never happen to me.

It took a minute, but the elevator finally reached the 23rd floor. The doors opened and the guard exited first before we were allowed to do so. The area that we stood in was pretty tight and it was about 10 of us in the group. The guards gave their signals and entry was given to proceed into the visiting room. We got a stamp prior to coming upstairs that indicated that we were visitors and instructed to confirm those stamps under a fluorescent light. We all were cleared to enter and given assigned seats. The inmates were not allowed to come from the back until we were seated. My seat was near the vending machine in the back of the room. I sat down and sat my money down on the seat next to me. The chairs were hard and plastic connected to each other so the guards could keep a close watch on everyone. As the inmates exited the backroom, they were instructed to sit across from their visitor. As name and after name was called I was getting nervous that maybe I wouldn't be able to see him. Did they cancel his visit and I was just waiting on someone to deliver the bad news? There were so many hypothetical scenarios that crossed my mind that my legs started to shake. Finally, the back inmate door opened one last time and out came the love of my life. His six-foot, three-inch frame, brown milk skin, and deep dimples came walking towards me ready to greet me with the biggest hug. The inmates were allowed to embrace their visitor for a very short period of time no more than 30 seconds, but it felt like we hugged for hours. I ran into his arms and it's like I fell in love all over again.

The orange federal jump suit didn't distract me from the handsome man that I had grown to love. He smelled like the finest cologne and his hair cut was the perfect shaped as if he just left the barbershop before the visit. The embrace comforted me like no other. I was in a safe space again and I never wanted to let that moment go. After a big hug and romantic kiss we both sat down and looked at each other for a few minutes just gazing. I could tell that he missed me, and I most definitely missed him. He left me in a vulnerable emotional state and I wasn't strong enough to handle it. He was my go to person for everything and as it stood he wasn't physically in my life at that moment and I had no clue when he was coming back home. He was a big part of my life, decision-making processes, and overall influence. So, I was ready to receive all of the information that I needed from him to be at ease. In that moment I needed reassurance. I didn't pray to God for the reassurance, I ran to him for it.

The first thing he said to me upon opening up the conversation was that everything was going to be okay. He went on to provide an example as to why things would be okay in the situation that took place in San Diego. The outcome of the case that he picked up did work in his favor after all. That conversation took away some of my anxiety in that moment, and I trusted him again. Because he was still on probation for what occurred in 1995, his federal probation officer had to get involved with extradition back to Chicago from San Diego. It was an immediate violation of his federal probation as a result of his early release from a 15-year sentence that spanned from the early 90's to around the time we met. The probation office wanted to violate him anyway due to the fact of him not having a job or being in school. She felt that he wasn't being a productive citizen and because of that wanted to send him back to jail. So, me being at a federal correctional facilities visiting room became inevitable.

He talked for an hour before he asked me to get him something to eat from the vending machine. I listened with mix feelings about why he made certain decisions. I still wasn't clear about why he decided to break the law. This is how I got exposed to who he really was and what he was actually involved with in the streets of Chicago. I had some suspicion about things but it started to be clear and evident on what it really was during his times of incarceration. I hung on to his every word. The conversations along with the case information that I was privilege to helped me come to a conclusion that maybe he had some involvement with the case. That very conclusion had me in a state of shock and nervous. In that moment I asked myself, who is this man? What did I get myself into? And did I have the courage to get myself out of it?

We had the most intriguing and intimate conversations while he was behind bars majority because he was forced to sit down. He was very limited to people and resources that he could use to his advantage. He was very dependent on me to take care of some of his legal business and communications during this time of being incarcerated. In turn, I felt honored to be able to assist him because I didn't have those privileges prior. I felt like he had left me in the dark about what was really going on with his legal trouble in the past, but now he had to let me in more. It bothered me for a while but I was too afraid to inquire about all of the details regarding the case in fear of how he would respond to me. So, I silenced my concerns and remained submissive. I also felt that maybe he had another woman helping him out. It was peculiar for him to not call me first as his woman to help out, whether it was calling his lawyer or gathering money for his bond. But this go around, I had an opportunity to really help out in any way that I could. It was an opportunity for me to show how responsible and resourceful I could be without depending and waiting on him to make a move.

The visitations lasted twice a week for three months. It took his federal probation officer some time to get him in court for the violation of his parole. I left work early on occasion and dedicated my weekends to spend time with him at the federal facility. The amount of money that I spent on parking, food, and commissary was not an issue for me at the time. I had a great salary at my job so that wasn't a problem for me. He also left a little bit of money to use in our account that helped out. I complied and did it proudly without any hesitation at all. He didn't have to worry about food or additional money to call me on a daily basis. I made it my duty to take care of his business without him having to tell me to do it. I honestly was enjoying the intimate moments of conversation that we were able to have during those visits. He expressed to me how much he was proud of me and because of my reaction to his legal trouble. I was going to be his wife one day soon – I just knew it in my heart. I smiled from ear to ear when he expressed those sentiments to me because I always wanted to know how he truly felt about our future together.

I had finally got him to the point of actually communicating with me, which was a huge accomplishment. After years of waiting and hoping for confirmation from him, I finally got it. That superseded all of the suspicion of cheating, staying out late, and not giving our relationship enough attention. I managed to get him out of his comfort zone, or at least I thought I did. He was very smart and strategic in the way in which he went about manipulating me. I was totally unaware of what he was doing but I later felt like I fell into his successful trap of manipulation.

Then I didn't realize how jail could really change a person's perspective on life and the people around them. I guess being back in jail made him dependent on others to take care of business and even help his case by any means necessary. Inmates have to send their friends and family visitation forms so the department can check their backgrounds in order for visits to be approved. While visiting him on a Saturday, another woman walked in the visiting room for him. We were having a conversation and his face turned red as the woman walked over to where we were sitting. The guards didn't know that the lady and I didn't know one another, so of course they allowed it to happen. He played it cool and told her to sit down beside me and introduced me as his woman. I was in a state of shock that he would even send another woman a visiting form to come and see him. I could not process what was happening in the moment so I sat silently as they went back and forth about whom I was and their relationship. Things concluded with her storming out of the visiting room vowing never to communicate with him again.

    I was left standing there after all of the shenanigans of another woman visiting my man. That incident was a topic of conversation for a couple of days that I eventually forgave him for and we moved on. He told me that he needed the woman for his case that he was fighting with the state. I felt betrayed and once again feelings of insecurities rose as a result. I thought, *how can this man do this from jail?* There I was sacrificing my time, money, and morals to make sure that he had everything he needed and once again I had questions about his loyalty to me. It took some time for me to get over it, but I eventually did. The love that I had for him trumped it all, and we moved on, together.

The legal trouble in California that he received probation for was considered to be a violation on the state case, where he got pulled over, and the federal case that he was on parole for. At one point he was facing three different cases. I tried to piece everything together with the minimal information that I had to draw my own conclusions. It was difficult to understand and grasp because I never experienced anything close to what he was facing - fighting criminal cases and no knowledge of how the legal system worked. I did more of my own research and fact finding through his personal paperwork, phone, and notes to really understand the magnitude of what I was facing. *What did I get myself into? Can I handle it?* Again, I had to ask myself because I couldn't believe I was here. I started to question so many things as a result of what seemed to be coming to a head.

    The day finally came for yet another transfer to take place. He was done with his federal parole violation. The judge gave him two years for violating his parole orders for the trip to California and the charges he picked up as well. The judge also ordered him to be transferred back to the federal facility at the conclusion of his state case. He was to be extradited to Cook County jail to fight the pending case that he was out on a $20k cash bond for. This would be a completely different experience for me on every level. I was ready to do whatever it took to make sure he had support. It didn't matter if he was guilty or not, he groomed me to withstand the severity of whatever needed to be handled. I learned how to control my feelings and reactions in any intense situation.

It took a few days for the state to pick him up to transport him from downtown Chicago to 22nd street, where Cook County Jail was located. The processing and cell assignment also took some time. That gave me some time to send him money on commissary and set up the phone. I became very familiar with the process at that point and knew what needed to happen. Their visitation process was very different from the federal system and didn't entail me filling out and submitting a form for approval. I knew that the experience would be different and not as personal and intimate because the Cook County jail is where anyone who is arrested for any crime in the county goes.

The population is huge and the facilities are overcrowded due to hefty bails amounts that most people can't afford. Often times, inmates have to sit until their case concluded, which could take years to happen. I had never been to the facility and I wasn't looking forward to it. I knew what to expect because he already debriefed me on the fact that I wouldn't be able to touch him, kiss, or hug him. We would be able to see each other but behind a glass and we would have to use a telephone to communicate. I was nervous about it but I knew that I had to shake it off because we were a step closer to him coming home. The outcome of the case in California and the federal violation were minimal. I could handle being away from him for a few months to a year to satisfy the federal probation violation sentencing.

It took him about a week to get settled before I was able to visit. We spoke on the phone before I made the trip up there, but we were only able to talk for 15 minutes as opposed to the longer visiting time at the federal facility. We talked about the remaining case that he was preparing and the details of what was needed in order for the outcome to work in his favor. As I listened things started to make sense as to why he reached out to the ex-girlfriend who showed up to the jail during my visit at the federal facility. He needed her help with the case that included some violence that prosecutors allege that he did. He was very strategic in the way he handled his business and the people around him. Every move he made was similar to a chess move. It was very interesting and mind blowing for me to witness and experience. It made me feel very uneasy, yet I listened and complied with every request because, at the end of the day, I belonged to him.

It was time to make the trip up to the Cook County jail for our visit. As I parked my royal blue Cadillac Escalade on the street, anxiety started to build. All I could think about was how this can't be my life right now. How did he end up at the point of incarceration? I never saw this as my reality whatsoever. Nevertheless, I had to save face for him. He needed to know that I had his back no matter what, right or wrong. So I took a deep breath, put the truck in park, and walked to the intake building. As I got close to the building, I noticed there was a line to enter for visitors. Everyone in line seemed very angry and impatient. There were people of different races there to visit their loved ones. The guards were rude and unforgiving. If a visitor didn't meet the clothing requirement or other infractions, they were quickly turned around and sent home to try again.

The Cook County guards moved and worked at their own pace often times ignoring people in line waiting to be taken care of. The process was very tense and tested my patience. When I got to the front of the line, I didn't have any issues or kick back from the guards. I passed the appropriate clothing test, cleared the metal detectors, and headed to the next building where he was housed. The walk was very uncomfortable as I listened to inmates hit the gates with their fist in hopes of getting the attention of the female visitors who walked to the different buildings to see their loved ones. I felt like a piece of meat as I walked in six inch heals with a fast pace to see him. I felt like a character in my own nightmare. I said to myself, this cannot be real. Never in a million years would I have envisioned myself taking trips to a prison multiple times in a week to see someone that I was madly in love with. Yes, I was out of my comfort zone, but optimistic about where we were headed. I checked in with my head held high in another prison facility and already I felt overwhelmed and spiritually drained.

    The intake process took almost an hour just to get a 15-minute visit with him. The federal process visitation lasted for four hours with snacks available for visitors to purchase. I had to go to one of the maximum security prison facilities where he was housed. All violent offenders with an extensive background were housed at a maximum building. It was clear that cleaning wasn't something that Cook County invested resources in. The doors were dirty, I was scared to touch the bathroom knob to relieve myself, and the glass that we had to speak to the inmates through had a smell that was unbearable to withstand.

By the time they called my name and went back to wait on him, the visit was almost over. I was anxious to see him and nervous to be there. I didn't like the stares or the uncomfortable energy that I experienced. I didn't fit in. Not that I felt like those people were beneath me. I knew that traveling from prison to prison wasn't my purpose, but I really didn't have much of a choice. It wasn't my destination, but I couldn't let him down. I needed to be different. Not for me though, but for him. I had no identity and I wasn't conscious of what was really going on. His word was law in my life and I had to follow him without question.

After about 30 minutes of waiting patiently, he walked in from the bullpen area to the window in front of me where a thick bulletproof glass separated us. We were not able to touch each other, hug, or do anything else that we had the opportunity to do in the federal facility. We had to communicate through a glass in which the other visitors had to as well. The environment was very noisy and distracting. I was uncomfortable throughout the entire time, but I managed to get through it.

We conversed about his plan to expedite the process of his release from the facility. He couldn't receive another bond amount due to the violations he received from the other cases. The information that I got from him was very specific as far as what he needed me to do with his lawyer. He made sure that I had his undivided attention because I had to remember everything that he told me. I would take notes when I got back to the truck because it was so much information that he fed me in a 15-minute time span and I was not allowed to bring paper and pencil inside the facility with me. Suddenly the guard instructed us that our time was up and we had to leave the facility to allow the next group an opportunity to visit their loved ones.

When I got back to the truck, I thought about everything that I needed to do for him regarding his case. The first thing that I did the next day was reach out to his lawyer to get the bail money transferred from the Cook County bail office to use as payment for his lawyer. This was important because his bail was retracted due to the case in California, which is why he was extradited back to the county jail and not kept at the federal facility downtown. I called his lawyer's office at work to set everything up and made sure that he had his contact information so that he could assist with the case immediately.

Initially, I didn't understand the severity of the case. When he was arrested as a result of the traffic stop, he didn't share full details of the charges that he faced at the time. There was information that was omitted from me. There was information that I found out from communicating with the layer. Case information that I was privy to prompted me to ask more questions about the particulars of what was going on with his case. I couldn't ask those questions over the phone, but our face-to-face visits were an opportunity for me to get more information about the severity of the case. He finally told me that he was facing a maximum of about 35 years in prison. My heart dropped as he went on to share the information of what happened and the result of a bad decision that he made with a friend. I had mixed feelings. I felt lies were told and it impacted the way that I looked at our relationship. I thought about the worst case scenario instead of best case because he was already in jail at that point. He made it his business to reassure me that all will be well with the cases and our future together as a couple. He reassured me that one day we would get married and start a family.

I finally trusted his word and did not question what would happen and the possible demise as a result of the case. So I complied. I spent my time coordinating things with his lawyer, he expected me to be at every visit on time ready to hear the task for the week and follow-up on what needed to be done for the case to get him a step closer to coming home. As time progressed, and I started to get more insight I got nervous. He was serious about challenging his case in front of a jury of his peers as an effort to come home immediately. He was really savvy with the system and predicted a lot with how things could possibly go with his case. The lawyer was only a tool for him to use in his plan to get the best possible deal that he could get. There were factors that would impact the outcome of his case related to his background, witnesses who could testify against him, and the buy-in from his lawyer could help him.

Observing the dynamic of what was going on with his case, the lawyers, and the risk, I recommended that it would probably be in his best interest to take a plea deal from the State of Illinois. I said it out of fear because the worst case would've equated to a lengthy jail sentencing from the prosecutor. I felt like he couldn't risk it because things could go either way. It wasn't about him, but about us in that moment. I feared prison for 25 years as being a possible outcome. All things would've been taken into consideration including the evidence from his background. With so many negatives stacked against him, I did not want to gamble with a longer sentence. The federal violation was settled, along with the out of town case that he picked up. I was ready to move on with my life and throw in the towel on the state case so we could move on.

The formalities of being in jail and the back end process that went along with it seemed like a game of chess to everyone involved. The prosecutors knew the lawyers and public defenders. It appeared that they went out after work to have drinks and talk about their cases to decide how things would go. I felt that the lawyers, judges, and prosecutors had not a care in the world about the inmates and how the sentencing would have a dramatic impact on families. That was the vibe that I experienced while visiting Cook County and the federal jails. It made me so uncomfortable to experience that and I wanted to make sure that he was good. So I was surprised that he agreed to take deal that the prosecutors negotiated with his lawyer. It was bitter sweet because jail time would be involved and he would be incarcerated for a period of time.

We spoke about the plea deal that was arranged by the prosecutor and his lawyer. Ending the pursuit of a trial saved the State of Illinois money, his lawyer, and other resources that would have gone into a full trial, had he made the decision to go that route. It became official. His lawyer delivered his deal that included four years of jail time with the possibility of parole with a guilty plea. That meant with good behavior and his participation in rehabilitation programs he could be home in two years.

He explained how one could navigate the system to come home earlier some time ago. That information matched everything that his lawyer and the prosecutor outlined in the paperwork. Taking the deal also was indicative of guilt on his end and became a solid finding on his record of charges of vehicle hijacking and kidnapping. I'm still not clear to this day if he had any involvement, other than allowing his friend to use his van on that day. He told me that he had nothing to do with anything detailed in the case. I believed him and moved on with mentally preparing for his departure from the city. It was a process before he was designated to a facility. All inmates had to go through a transitional facility called Statesville in downstate Illinois. He estimated that once he departed from Cook County that it would be another month before he was processed and in a position to reach out to me.

    I was able to visit him a few more times at the Cook County jail before he had to leave and make his transition to another facility. I met with his lawyer to pick up a check for $25,000. This was the remaining balance of the bond that he paid when he was booked after the traffic stop and his lawyer fee. He told me that the money would be cushion for us to use when he came home. It was our savings so we could start over. The experience had drawn us closer than we've ever been prior to him being incarcerated. It appeared to me that he was ready for bigger and better things including marriage, home, and children. I was elated to hear him speak about our future plans together. I needed to feel that security in our relationship because I was insecure about my position in the relationship due to other women that I suspected he was seeing. I wanted and had to be his number one, and I felt like I had reached that point with the recent events of his legal trouble.

He was transferred to Statesville Correctional Facility where he was held for approximately three weeks before being transferred yet again to a medium correctional facility in Canton, Illinois. Canton was about three hours always from Chicago. While I waited for his phone call, I again made sure that he had money on hand so he could buy the things he needed from commissary and money to call me. By the time he was locked up in Canton, I was used to the process and protocol of what needed to be done from the federal and state facilities. He always had the necessary resources to survive in prison.

I never dealt with the reality of him going away. I was at ease knowing that everything was over in terms of fighting the case. I knew that it was an uphill battle at that point. In my mind, two years wasn't bad at all. We were going through the court cases and dealt with different facilities for six months, so another 18 months or so didn't hurt. He made sure to confirm that the sentencing was the best thing that happened to us and we had dodged a bullet in the process. I made a conscious decision to wait on the man I loved. I wanted to show him that I could be his wife. I wanted him to know that this wasn't an opportunity for me to seek a new man or relationship. I was committed to him and nothing else mattered. So, I dedicated my mind and spirit to making sure that I was present for him while he was doing his time. I wanted him to know that he had my full support and I wouldn't let anything stop that. Being a part of the process made me feel important and that we were in a serious relationship. I wanted so much to be a huge part of his life and not just existence and being someone he took care of, which is how I felt for a long time.

    After waiting for a few weeks, the moment finally arrived. He had checked out of Statesville Correctional Center and transferred to Canton where he was schedule to complete the rest of his time. The journey would take a couple of days for him to get in the system and housed in a location on the prison grounds. I started mapping it immediately how I would make my travel to him. I was slightly unsure of what our visitation schedule would be, so I waited patiently for his call. He reached out to me after a few days and we spoke about the plan to get me on the visiting list to see him immediately. We came to the conclusion that I would drive every other week to Canton during my pay schedules. He didn't want me to touch the $25k that we had in savings. He made plans on how to make that money grow upon his release. The drive was a few hours away so I rented cars from Midway Airport in Chicago to avoid putting miles on my Cadillac Escalade.

  I couldn't wait to get out there and see him the week after my visit was approved with the facility. I was anxious to visit him. I was used to seeing him every week either at the federal prison or Cook County building. It was a strange feeling that I was kind of getting acclimated to. It became a remote relationship.

Subconsciously, I didn't want my current state to be my new normal. Although, I rolled with motions with ease, I still would have moments that I couldn't believe that this was the life I was living. I felt like I had fallen into a trap that I couldn't get myself out of. I was deeply in love with someone whose lifestyle consisted of something that I knew nothing about and it's like he was hiding it from me.

It became clear to me that he was either big time drug dealer or had a very large roll in drug activity. I retrieved that information from the public records indicated on the prison website when I completed my personal background check on him. There was no evidence of him still being involved in that lifestyle but there was so much that was kept from me in effort to protect myself. I felt that he lied and hid the truth from me because he knew that it would scare me and I would probably leave the relationship.

REFORM'D

The time came for me to pack my bag and head to Canton. I had a set routine where I would visit on a Sunday and stay the entire visitation block (which was about six hours). Visits would start at 9am and end at 3pm. I drove with no problem listening to my music and talking to my best friend on the phone gossiping about the week. My adrenaline was so high that the drive didn't bother me. The excitement would build from the thought of being able to touch and see him again.

I hadn't been able to touch him since our visitation at the federal facility in downtown Chicago. My initial visit with him was filled with kisses, hugs, and deep conversations. It went from planning on his end to relief that it was all over. The case in San Diego resulted to parole and a fine, the federal probation violation resulted in two years, and the case that weighed the heaviest was with the State of Illinois that involved vehicular kidnapping and other miscellaneous charges that sent him to Canton with a four year sentence.

For us that meant that it was over and we could move on with planning the next phase of our lives together. I envisioned it to be happier times, marriage, and a child. I knew that we were finally at the point in our relationship where we could really be together like a normal couple. Our visits were simply about how we would grow the money that was on hand in savings and live our best lives no matter what. He was adamant about marriage and starting a family. Often he would express how he considered me to be a soldier because I was able to withstand everything we had going on.

Those moments of intimate interactions made me feel like his wife. It made me happy and excited about our future together. I was serious about doing what was necessary to please him. It was never about me. My identity didn't exist, and I had no clue that I was in the relationship. It was all about his direction and vision for the relationship. My spirit was broken as a result, but I didn't let him see that from me. In my mind, love trumped everything.

So the visits continued for two years. Every other Sunday it would be the same routine of me renting a car to drive three hours to see him. There were good conversations and bad ones. We had some funny moments and intense conversations. It was important for me to see him. I know that it made him feel a sense of security knowing that I would always be there for him. Throughout his time there he was also able to get involved into some programs that would decrease his incarceration time drastically. Those programs included obtaining his GED and spending time learning about a trade. He decided to take up the barber trade. He quickly got the sentence reduced from four years to two years.

We made plans for everything that we were going to do together from our living situation to having our first child. It was exciting to know that we were on the same page regarding how we wanted to live. Those discussions took place over a game of chess and snacks that I bought from the vending machine for him to eat. He looked forward to the food in the vending machine as oppose to what they fed him in the prison kitchen at the facility. We had grown so close over the duration of his prison time. It felt so good to have him on the same page with me willing to support the relationship at all costs. I was worried on some occasions and thought to myself, *what if all of this is an act to just keep me close and things would be different when he got home?* My friends, who at some point experienced incarceration with the men in their lives, told me stories of such things happening to them. The

REFORM'D

thought of it made me nervous but I was willing to give him a fair shot at living life right with me.

Chapter 5 – A Chance for New Life

The day finally came for him to check out and officially come home to start life on the right path. He met with the parole board to review whether or not he would be approved for parole. The meeting went well and the parole was approved with the condition that he would meet with his parole officer once a month to check in with an officer on job search and drug/alcohol consumption. The drug and alcohol testing weren't a problem because he didn't engage in any of those activities. He always told me that he needed to be alert when interacting with different people, especially on the streets of Chicago. In addition, he passed the GED test, and he went through a rehabilitation program, which helped dramatically. All of the extracurricular activities were strategies for him to get home sooner and it worked. I thought to myself that he really was an expert and knew exactly how the system worked in his favor. Whatever he told me that was related to his case played out exactly how he said it would. I was impressed with how knowledgeable he was and how strategic he could be in any situation. I never saw him panic about anything and it made me confident and trustworthy of the outcome of his case.

    I couldn't sleep because I was very excited for him to come home. I made sure that my bags were packed and ready for the ride to Canton for the last time. He requested the day before that I bring $10,000 with me on the trip to have in his pocket. There was a project that he needed to work on immediately following his release of being home. He assured me that it was an investment project that he was working on and that it would put us in a position to buy a home and pay off some debt we both had.

He also requested that I bring him a change of clothes as well. He didn't want to wear prison clothes outside at all. I made sure that his bag was packed as well for the trip.

Instead of the usual three hours on the road, it took me two hours to get to the facility. It was very sunny outside with warm temperatures. My music played through the speakers of the Chevy Malibu that I rented for the trip. I really got a great view of the mountains and I truly felt like this was it. The old things were in the past and we were ready to move on to bigger and better things together. I was at peace with the past and ready to move forward. One of our last conversations on the phone was how we were going to have a baby soon after his release. I went as far as getting an ovulation kit to monitor the time period that I was ovulating. Coincidently, I took a test before leaving for the trip and as I suspected, I was in ovulation territory. I didn't let him know that because I knew he would make a big deal out of it and push to try for a baby. I never told him, but in the past my doctor told me that I would have some difficulties with conceiving due to some hormonal imbalance. A routine doctor visit with my gynecologist turned into running some emergency tests, which later determined that I'd require help conceiving a child in the future. It concerned me a little because I knew that marriage and children were something I desired. At that moment, I was young and enjoying life. I took the news and put it back in my subconscious. I told my mother about what the doctor told me about my hormones and I let it go.

As I walked in the facility, I looked around for the last time. This was it for us. No more long trips to Canton, bearing the harsh smell and filth of Cook County, or the disgruntled government workers of the federal prison system. I was there to pick him up from the facility and we were going to ride off into the sunset together as a new and improved couple who had been through some things that changed their relationship and connection for life. Initially, I was told that I had arrived too early and to return after 11:00 am. I accepted that news because I thought that the officer wanted to deliver some bad news about his release. With the number of transfers and cases that he fought I was a little nervous that something else would stop him from coming home. So I decided to go down the road to a local restaurant to sit and have coffee as I anxiously watched my clock and waited for the clock to strike 10:45. At that time, I got in the car and drove back down the road to the facility and waited in the parking lot for another 10 minutes. At the 11:00 hour, I walked into the building and was instructed by the officer to sit and wait for him to come out. So I waited patiently for another two hours and watched as people reconnected with their loved ones who had been incarcerated for some time. I watched as others came in to visit their loved ones who were not being released, but still had time to serve. I felt bad for them because they had to watch our loved ones get released from the same prison where their loved ones were still incarcerated.

To my surprise, after a long two hours, he came walking from the back of the prison facility to the main intake facility to be processed out. His face lit up with joy as I stood there in his favorite bomber black jacket, black leggings, and knee length boots ready to embrace him. He could not stop smiling at the sight of me. After he read off the numbers to the officer, the handcuffs were unlocked and he was free from incarceration. We hugged for about 10 minutes and hurried up and made our exit from the building. We wanted to get far away from that place as possible. He couldn't stop hugging and kissing me, and I enjoyed every minute of it. When we got to the car we immediately went to the trunk of the car to get his clothes so that he could change. I packed a brown duffle bag for him with a jogging suit, gym shoes, and the $10,000 as he requested. He smiled from ear to ear at me. I'd imagined the feeling of freedom was exhilarating. For me, I had my man back. He was my protector, my confidant, and my hero.

    He decided to drive back home and I had no problem with that, besides he hadn't been behind a wheel in two years and I was tired from the drive that I had to commit to on a bi-weekly basis. He got into the driver's seat and we drove off. The ride back reminded me of Bonnie and Clyde. We had the music blasting as he drove the Illinois highways. The feeling was great but that fear of the unknown seeped right back in. What was his plan to make money? The incarceration trend scared me and I wanted to be confident that he was home to stay forever. I didn't want to go back through what I just experienced with him in prison.

He had a plan to get things rolling immediately once we touched down in Chicago. As we got closer to the city I could tell that he was so excited to be back at home. We had a plan to stop at LA Fitness to activate our gym memberships and then head over to Best Buy to get some electronic devices. The day was filled with spontaneity and I loved every minute of it. I finally was in a position where I said to myself that this is what a relationship was about. It was a feeling that I longed for with him. I wasn't sure if I would ever get it until that moment. I smiled and was present in the moment. I noticed that he was different as a result of his recent incarceration. I was convinced that he was a changed man for the better. He was very attentive to my needs and wanted to please me in every way.

I didn't even have to take public transportation to and from work anymore. See in Chicago when you work in the downtown area it's easier and cheaper to take the train or bus to work because of parking restraints. Charlie was present and made me feel like I was truly indeed his woman. I knew that we were on a different wave in our relationship and I felt like I had his commitment no matter what. It was planned for us to live our best lives and the path we were taking meant that we were about to embark on an amazing path together. That awesome feeling lasted for about two months. The savings account that he promised would be used for real estate, started to dwindle and I had no clue where the money was going. I was scared to ask questions because it was technically his money, not ours. I trusted his planning and strategic moves with everything so I kept my cool.

However, things weren't adding up and the plans that we both agreed upon were not playing out the way we hoped. He started to revisit old habits of being secretive, disappearing in the middle of the night, and withholding information from me.

I felt insecure and uneasy at the fact that he was taking us backwards in the relationship. It became harder for me to get through to him. He was unreasonable and stubborn in his ways. Because of those actions, I knew that he was in a desperate mindset and clearly he had a goal in mind that he wanted to achieve and he was going to achieve it no matter what. He promised me while he was incarcerated that he would communicate with me much better than he had. The conversation that I had with friends had seemed to be true. He started to be a completely different person at home than who he was while in prison. While being away, he seemed to be so attentive and depended on me to take care of so much of his business. Now he was making all of the decisions and no longer communicating with me.

After a while, I decided to put my focus back on myself and work. I had a sales position where accountability was very intense. Working out was a way for me to realign my mind, body, and spirit. I decided to no longer put all of my attention on him and the things he was doing. I would leave work and go three blocks away to workout at a gym. It was my mission to keep myself occupied so that I could keep my mind off of him and what he was doing during that time. He picked me up when he wasn't too busy running the streets. I would ask questions only to be disregarded and lied to. The reasoning he gave me sounded like they were lies. But I never wanted to get into an argument with him so I left a lot of things alone.

I hoped for things to change with the course of our relationship. One of our plans that we discussed while he was incarcerated was to have a child and get married when he came home. Although, I knew we would have challenges, I was ready to take on the challenge - anything to attempt to refocus Charlie's vision. Initially, when the doctor told me about the issues that she had found during my test, I didn't care and was okay with the information that she had given me because it worked in my favor that I couldn't get pregnant. I didn't tell him about the issue because I didn't want him to be alarmed about me not being able to have kids with him. But now that I needed something to distract him, getting pregnant seemed like the best option seeing that things had changed. Although, I attempted to distract myself in the gym it just wasn't working and I needed something else.

One Monday morning I was at my desk at my new job when my body was overwhelmed with the feeling of being sleepy and exhausted. I thought that it was from me going so hard in the gym just weeks prior. My mind went back to the day that I picked him up from the prison and the ovulation test that I took was positive, meaning I was indeed ovulating the same day that he came home.

After experiencing the exhaustion for a few weeks, I decided to go to the local drug store and buy a pregnancy test. I didn't want to tell him until I was sure whether I was pregnant or not. The local CVS was about 10 minutes away from my apartment. I went straight to the store and bought two tests and drove home. My body was numb from the anxiety and nerves that I experienced during that short time. He wasn't home so that was perfect timing for me to take the test to determine the results. As I sat on the back of the toilet in my bathroom, my thoughts were conflicting because I wanted to start a family with him, but I knew that financially we weren't ready and our relationship status was shaky at that point.

I continued on with the process as those thoughts were looming in my head. The stick sat on the sink for about 30 seconds as I waited for the results to come back showing that I was in fact pregnant. The results put me in a state of shock because in my heart, I believed that I was pregnant. In denial, I took the second test that also came back positive for pregnancy. I thought to myself, *what am I to do now*? I knew that I needed to tell him about it. My initial thought was that he would be happy that I was pregnant. I knew that our relationship was not in the best place but having a family was something that he wanted, without a doubt.

I picked up my cell phone and called him. He was on the road driving in his pick-up truck that he bought upon his return from prison. I told him the result of the test and he was indeed excited about being a father. After he got off the phone with me, he was home within an hour max. Our negativity and differences were replaced by joy and excitement at the thought of having a baby. In my mind, I thought that having a child would make things better between us. God had blessed me with the opportunity to conceive at 28 years of age after hearing my doctor tell me that it would be difficult for me to conceive. We cuddled in my queen size bed for the rest of the night. It felt good, and I felt comforted the entire night in his arms. There was no other place that I wanted to be. I didn't contact my family that night. I wanted to cross that bridge on a different day because that night was special for us and it was important that we cherished it.

During my eight months of pregnancy, he treated me like a queen of his universe. I could tell that he was so excited about the journey that we were about to embark upon. He wasn't a man that showed many emotions at all and he opted often times to remain mute and focused on what was going on around him.

I knew that he was happy from the smiles and generous gestures on a daily basis from him. I didn't have to lift a finger and everything that I wanted I got from him. He made sure that we went shopping for maternity clothes often. I stayed in the most comfortable gym shoes. He wanted to make sure that I was comfortable at all cost. He went the extra mile to make sure that I was okay. It was something we both wanted and we were ecstatic about the opportunity to be parents, especially considering my hormones not being in sync.

I was confident that this new journey in our lives would change our relationship forever. He seemed ready to take on a new life with me as a family man.

The disappointment and resentment that I felt for him prior to finding out about the pregnancy quickly went away. It was time for us to become one and transition into parents for the sake of our unborn child. I felt like it took us to get pregnant for him to realize that the most important thing in life was about family and peace. The sense of security was on the horizon for us. Besides, this would be his first child and having a family would give him an opportunity to do everything with his child that his father didn't do with him.

When the shock and excitement wore off, I noticed that his focus began to shift back to the mode of making money to be able to provide for our future family. The reality of our situation was that I was bringing home a consistent paycheck every two weeks, but it wasn't enough to live exactly like we were accustomed to. As a result of his most recent incarceration, we consolidated our living arrangements and we moved him out of his Northside condo that he rented. He used majority of the savings that I set to the side when I received his bail money back from the lawyer to invest in a personal project that he promised would put us in a better financial position before the baby's arrival. I trusted his word and knew that he wouldn't let me down. He always kept his promise and anything that he discussed with me, whether it was in regards to paying a bill for me or taking care of a business concern, he took care of it without question or hesitation.

My worry and stress levels increased as I progressed in pregnancy. There were secondary bills that were behind and we were still in my one bedroom apartment and dependent solely on my income from my job. There was no way that I could take care of three people. I didn't discuss my feelings with him. I kept everything inside and simply trusted his word about how he would figure everything out. As a result of the stress of our unstable financial situation, I was stressed and was under the threat of a miscarriage.

While home one evening watching television on the couch, my bladder was full to capacity, and I needed to use the restroom. The pressure was stronger than usual, so I knew there was something wrong. I ran to the bathroom and as soon as I sat down on the toilet, urine and lumps of blood came out of me. I immediate thought that I lost my baby at three months. There was no pain, only blood clots. I immediately started crying hysterically and screamed out the name of Jesus. I refused to move, I didn't want to look and see what was in the toilet. In my mind, I knew that my baby was floating in the water. I never felt so afraid in my life. It was like my soul had left my body and my life was over. Everything around me seemed to stop. I held my breath for a few seconds and put my head in my hands. I started to blame myself. I blamed the incident on the fact that I was training to ensure that I maintained a healthy weight during the pregnancy, which in my mind was the reason why I was in that predicament. It felt like my whole life was over. The blessing behind knowing that I was expecting a child gave me so much hope and motivation in my life.

He was the first person I called. When he picked up the telephone, I couldn't get the words out to tell him what took place. With heavy breathing and stuttering over my words, I told him to come back to the house because I lost the baby. He immediately hung up the phone after our brief conversation asking no questions. Next, I called my mother crying uncontrollably to tell her what was going on. She prayed with me on the phone, and I told her that I didn't feel pregnant anymore and that I think I lost the babe. She asked me if I wanted her to come over, but I refused. I wanted Charlie and I to deal with the reality of me losing the baby. I told her that I would give her a call back upon my arrival to the hospital.

After waiting 20 minutes or so, I heard the shuffling of keys at the front door. I sat on the toilet naked and in he came storming rushing to get to the bathroom to check on me. I slowly lifted my head and told him that we lost the baby, and I messed up. He helped me up and looked in the toilet where there was an extremely large amount of blood and clots floating. I could tell that he was worried. I saw a look on his face that I never seen before. He helped me put on my clothes and we drove to the local hospital about 15 minutes away from the apartment. The drive was somber and silent. There were so many thoughts going through my mind. I felt like losing my baby meant I had nothing else to offer him. Our first child was gone and because of stress and my intense workouts, I ruined that chance for the both us. Losing his first-born would send him back to the streets instead of being the family man that I desired him to be. My eyes stared at the street lights and movement of traffic. I was in a daze of no return. Life as I knew it was over in my mind.

When we arrived at the hospital, I explained the situation to the nurses and they quickly rushed us to the back for further tests to be completed. Charlie tried to uplift my spirits as much as he could, but it didn't work. I even saw him praying which was surprising to see. He never prayed in my presence so that let me know that he was serious about family life. The head doctor notified us that we had to go to the back for an ultrasound. I had no clue why because there wouldn't be anything to see in my uterus. He decided not to go in the back with me and I was okay with that decision. The nurses rolled my bed to the back room where the warm equipment stood waiting. I wasn't conscious of what was going on around me because I kept tormenting and blaming myself for the incident. I was in a soulless state of mind. The nurse explained the procedure that needed to happen with the process. When she inserted the vaginal stick inside me, I looked up at the lights shaking uncontrollably from my nerves and anxiety. When she positioned the stick, I saw her reach over to turn the monitor on and after a few adjustments I heard the loud sound of a strong heartbeat from a small fetus. My baby was still alive! There was a rush of joy and energy that filled my soul as a result.

    The nurse rolled me back to the lobby area where Charlie was waiting and we celebrated together. I gave God all thanks for allowing our baby to survive. Before leaving, the doctor told us that I was still at risk and needed to take it easy and see my regular doctor that following week. Charlie went above and beyond to make sure that I had everything I needed that entire weekend. I was confined to my couch where he provided all of the snacks that I needed and the remote control was right next to me. He demanded that I didn't move or put myself at risk at all to lose our baby, and I complied.

    I didn't have any more issues after that and the rest of the time that was left during my pregnancy was successful. That incident allowed us to grow closer as a couple and there was nothing that could stop us because we just experienced the greatest fear that put us at the most vulnerable state of our relationship at that time. I felt like the incident had exposed his softer side, which I rarely got to experience. There was nothing that could get in the way of us being great parents to our child. His heartbeat represented strength to me and there was nothing that we were unwilling to endure to make sure that we were one for our child. I knew that God was looking out for us and he even acknowledged that he was definitely looking out for us as well.

I delivered a healthy baby boy. It didn't take long for me to push him out of my uterus. The entire process took no more than a few hours. His mother and my best friend were there. They cheered me on in labor and delivery. My son came out with the umbilical cord wrapped around his neck and fighting. I couldn't hold him immediately. The staff took care of him for a few minutes to make sure that he was good before I had the opportunity to hold him. The process of giving birth to my handsome son was painful but those feelings faded when I heard him cry and saw his little face. I knew then that he was a blessing from God and I was excited and nervous about the journey ahead.

Chapter 6 –Desperate Times, Desperate Measures

We were ecstatic about the opportunity to raise our little boy. We discussed his future and the great things that we wanted for him as it related to his education and the molding that would be required to ensure that we would raise a man. The first five months of his life was an adjustment for us, but we were hands on in the learning process. He wanted to learn how to change his pamper and make a warm bottle. I breast fed for an extensive period of time so it wasn't a hard task for him to pick-up the techniques of warming up a bottle. In those moments of watching him, I could tell that he was very proud of being a parent and he was very serious about it. He wanted to be hands on with his doctor's appointments as well. I only took an eight-week maternity leave to care for our son because we needed the money. I did not have the option to stay home permanently and the short-term disability wasn't enough to take care of all of us, so I had to prepare to go back to work early. That was the reality of the situation and we both came to terms that something needed to change and fast. He promised that things would be different very soon and to give him a minute to figure things out. I complied, but I also told him that I could be of assistance in planning for us to secure a bigger apartment until we were ready to purchase a home. He insisted that everything would be okay, and he just wanted me to focus on caring for our son.

  He had no interest regarding my ideas and what I could contribute to help make our situation better. Things got very stressful and tensed in our relationship because of our financial state. I didn't understand why he would risk all of the money we saved on a project that never generated income for our family as promised. In my mind, we could've shifted the money elsewhere to ensure that we had more than one bedroom for our child and could live and be comfortable until we were ready to make our next move. In addition, I had no details about the unspoken project only speculation as to what he was doing and hoped that it would work for our family.

    My mother volunteered to watch our son when I went back to work until we were comfortable with a daycare facility. Her decision to take over was a heavy load off of me because I was very nervous about putting him in a daycare. We created a routine with my mother regarding our drop off and pick-up schedule and everything worked out according our plan. As time progressed, I noticed a shift. Charlle was starting to fall back to old habits. He was starting to become predictable in this way. After dropping Evan and I off, he would stay out late and did not return home sometimes until 3:00 – 4:00 in the morning. I noticed the secret phone conversations and multiple cell phones that were in his possession. My anxiety levels started to rise as I felt like he was back in the streets doing things that contradicted everything that we planned for our family. In that moment, our relationship was changing and it resorted back to the way it was before he went back to prison. My feelings of uncertainty and instability started to hit me hard. This time was different because I also had a baby to care for, so I could not allow myself to stay in that state for a long period of time.

    I tried to speak with him about it and reason with him regarding the direction that I felt we were going in, but he refused to speak on it. He assured me that he had everything figured out. I was angry that once again I was left out of making important decisions for our family. He expected me to sit back and simply wait on him to make something happen. He wanted me to trust his word as I've done on plenty occasions. This time was different because it seemed that everything that he was getting his hands on was failing dramatically. He kept losing money in savings and investments that he made with other people. He started to get angry and desperate at the hard times we were experiencing.

I could tell that his ego was starting to take a hit, too because he couldn't deliver on the promises that he'd made to me as he has done before and it negatively affected him. The pressure was on heavier than before because of our child. I continued to work making about $45k a year at my job to support our household that included three people and bills that were becoming past due because we couldn't afford to pay them. Eventually, essential bills were not getting paid. I started to feel anxious and angry because I felt that we were in a tough spot because of the decisions he made to handle our money the wrong way and without having a conversation with me about his plans to invest and spend it.

As the days and months went by, the tension between us continued to grow. There were some tough decisions we had to make as a result of us needing to provide for Evan. He was able to make some things happen on occasion for the household, but nothing consistent. I tried to convince him that he needed to find a job and just work to bring in a consistent check, but he refused.

He continued to stay out late and leaving us at home alone. It brought back old insecurities that I thought went away considering what we had gone through with him being incarcerated. That was a major problem for me. We still had our daily routine that included dropping Evan off in the morning and then he would drop me off at work. After that, he had the entire day to himself to do anything he wanted because I didn't get off work until 7:00 pm. The infidelity surfaced again which included late conversations and I found random numbers in his phone. There were nights that he didn't come home at all. He was driving their cars and lied and said that they belonged to friends. I would check the registrations only to learn that other women owned them. I drove to dangerous neighborhoods looking for him only to learn that he was cuddling with other women at their homes. Witnessing first-hand what he was doing to our family made me respond different than before. At that point, I knew that I wanted out. My son had given me enough courage and worth in life that it was time for me to move on. I remember telling myself that God had more for me. My life as it stood had taken a toll on my strength and I couldn't take it anymore.

I shut down emotionally, spiritually, and physically. I wanted nothing to do with him at all. I thought about everything that I had done and been through with him. He didn't get that I was ready to settle down, raise our son, and eventually get married. I started to remember the multiple jails bids, multiple women, and instability that finally took its toll on me. Change needed to happen immediately.

As a result of my actions and distance, he continued to take care of his son but wanted nothing to do with me. He slept on the couch in my living room, he continued to stay out to take care of *business* and refused to engage in conversation with me or give me an explanation of his actions. He felt that the bulk of issues stemmed from the state of our finances and his inability to do what he was able to do in the past. He wasn't prepared for the adjustment that was necessary for us to be a family and live life the right way.

Although I was very distant and planning my escape from him, I was very observant when he was around. There was something going on, but I had no clue to what it was about. He was very quiet around me and zoned out. There were times that he came home completely exhausted from being outside. We weren't communicating so I knew nothing. If it wasn't about Evan, I had absolutely nothing to say to him because of his actions and the status of our relationship. I was ready for my life to change after six years of being with him. I knew that leaving him would be difficult, but I was ready and willing to start over with my son.

On Saturday June 2, 2012 at approximately 3:00 am, I heard him come into my room dressed in all black. He thought I was asleep for the night but I heard and saw him. Our son was asleep as well in his basinet next to me. He walked over and gently kissed him on the forehead and before leaving the bedroom he knocked on the footboard and told me that he would be back later. It was something about that night that didn't feel right in my soul. I heard the front door close and he locked it. After about a minute, I jumped up and looked out my window to watch him leave the parking lot. We owned two cars at the time, a black pick-up truck and my 2005 Cadillac Escalade. We both had keys to both vehicles to use whenever necessary. He decided to take the Cadillac with him that early morning. Fortunately, I grabbed my baby's car seat and stroller out of the truck the day before. I planned on taking my son to work with me that very same day. I didn't want to, but I had a plan and needed extra money to move out.

    The same morning I got up around 7:30 am to get Evan and me ready for the day. I planned to work from 9am – 2pm and head to my mother's house afterward to relax with her. I had a feeling of uneasiness that entire morning as a result of him taking off so early. It was something different about that good bye that left me in a state of vulnerability. Once again, he left without telling me any information about where he was going and with whom. I was always in the dark about his whereabouts and business and it made me feel unimportant in our relationship. Taking my son to work with me wasn't ideal, but I felt compelled to take Evan with me to my workplace where I had my own office space.

  I tried calling him at 7:30 am that morning, but he did not answer. It didn't alarm me much because he was known not to pick up the phone but usually he would call me back to let me know everything was fine. I kept calling while I was in the process of getting dressed to go to work and even on the commute downtown, but to no avail. I became very concerned about his well-being especially since he got robbed just weeks prior on a deal that went bad. That was the story that he gave me. A group of men took about $20,000 of our savings. He said it was the money that he was going to use for investments. It was just a vicious cycle of us building up to only lose the money again.

    I knew the incident left him in a bad place. He was vengeful and angry at what happened, and he didn't bounce back from the robbery. My mind scanned through many scenarios of where he could possibly be. I figured there was a chance that he would either be at another woman's house or dead. The thoughts were bad outcomes to fathom considering I was a new mom at 28 years of age and scared about the journey ahead of me.

    I was on pins and needles at work while waiting on him to call me back. Hours passed by without me hearing anything from him and his whereabouts. Evan was irritable from being in the stroller all day at the job and my thoughts and feelings were numb. After hours waiting to hear back from him, he finally called me at approximately 2:00 in the afternoon. When his name popped up on my caller ID, I was very eager to answer it. My heart was filled with anticipation and nerves. I didn't say hello upon answering the call. My first question I asked him was whether or not he was okay. He responded but it wasn't a response that would answer my question. I heard him whisper to me that he was in trouble. I asked for him to repeat it. He did, and he went on to explain to me that he had gotten into some trouble that involved a bank robbery in a nearby suburb. I was shocked at what he told me and too numb to respond. He concluded the conversation and told me that he loved me and the baby, and that everything was going to be okay and he couldn't stay on the phone long.

He hung up before I could say anything in response to what took place. I began walking south on State Street in the downtown area of Chicago feeling defeated. I couldn't believe how my whole world changed in one day. All I could do was walk while pushing my son's stroller down State Street with no destination in mind. I felt like the world had stopped momentarily. I knew that life as I knew would be very different from that point moving forward. I went into a reactive state and called my mom to let her know what happened. Then I called his mother to inform her of what took place. She was in shock at what I told her and insisted that she would come downtown to pick us up.

During the interim of waiting for his mother to pick us up, he called back. The conversation included more details about what took place and the trouble that he had gotten himself into that day. The bank robbery turned into a manhunt due to his escape from the facility. The bank was robbed for a quarter of a million dollars. He didn't want to turn himself in to the authorities so he hid in the duct area of a nearby shopping mall. I immediately Googled the incident online to find out what was going on and if what he stated was true. There was an active report about the incident on a local web page in Chicago that had some basic information about the robbery. It wasn't a joke.

The events that were taking place were very real and I was being directly impacted by it. I was in a state of shock and disbelief at the moment. The first thought that came to mind was my son and how I would care for him on my own. What were we going to do? How can I survive without him? How much time would he have to serve? I had many questions but no answers.

It didn't take his mother long to get downtown. She picked Evan and me up from State Street. We got right in the van and headed to my apartment. We both sat quietly in the van at a loss for words. We were both disappointed in his actions and disgusted at the fact that he left his family to suffer from the consequences of his actions on that day. That day changed my life forever. His mother was directly impacted as well because he took care of her too.

    I called him on the drive home to check on him. He answered and I tried to convince him to stop hiding and turn himself in to the authorities. I didn't want the police to kill him since it was a manhunt for his capture. He insisted that everything would be okay and he wouldn't have to do much time in jail. He did everything he could to calm me down. I tried to calm down but it was too much to process in that moment. I had no car, a six-month old son, and parent responsibilities that I couldn't perform on my own.

REFORM'D

After his mother left the apartment, I sat in the middle of my living room floor and reflected on where my life was and the direction it was headed in. My apartment was about 800 square feet and the walls seemed like they were closing in on me. Immediately, depression started to set in my soul, and I was ready to give up on life. Doubt and fear crept up very fast. Thoughts and internal conversations begin to surface in my mind. Because of Evan, I knew I needed to snap out of it and leave the apartment. I planned to go to my mother's house because I had no access to a vehicle. He used the truck that he bought me for the baby to commit a crime. He owned a pick-up truck that was parked in the complex parking lot, but it needed some work. I had very little hope, and I needed to be around my mother who I knew would support me and love on me during the toughest time of my life.

When I arrived at my mother's house, she didn't ask any questions. She made sure that she had a meal prepared for me, my baby was taken care of, and that the extra bedroom was ready for Evan and me. I waited by the phone patiently for him to call me back but there was nothing for hours. The communication stopped between us and I didn't know if he was dead or alive. I decided to check my phone again for some information and the reports were everywhere. The headlines read: "Bank Robbery in Oak Lawn" plastered on every news website, both locally and nationally. He was finally captured after a 12-hour manhunt. The details read the $250,000 was stolen from the vault, employees were tied and bounded, and he was caught wearing a dreadlock wig to disguise himself. The stories also stated that he was caught after being stuck in an air duct for hours. I kept reading the articles, scrolling through Google searches, and crying out in the process. My life was over. I felt like I would be right back in a lifestyle of poverty and struggle. I messed up my life by making the wrong decisions that inevitably led me to be with the wrong man. I blamed myself and I felt that it was also a result of my disobedience. I deserved what was happening and I had no clue of how to deal with it. I wanted to give up, but I couldn't for the sake of my son. I owed him at least an effort to get through the traumatic experience of our lives changing within 24 hours.

    I didn't go to bed that night and I had to get up the next morning for work. My mother was accustomed to taking care of Evan so the routine continued. She even offered to let us stay there until things settled. I was still in a state of shock while commuting to work. I couldn't eat or think at all, but work kept me occupied. The federal authorities kept him housed at the federal facility located in downtown Chicago. It was the same facility that I visited when he violated his parole for the San Diego case. Since he got arrested over the weekend, his bond hearing didn't happen until that following Wednesday. I had no clue when I would be able to speak with him. I knew that everything had to be in place for him to make a phone call and that could take some time.

In preparation for his bond hearing, I got a call from his public defender that was assigned to him by the federal court. She asked questions about his past, family, and mental health to gather enough information to present a case where he could get house arrest. I knew that wouldn't be an option since he was a repeat offender. She asked if I was going to attend the preliminary hearing and I reluctantly said yes. At that point I still hadn't spoken to him since being captured by authorities.

The preliminary hearing at the federal courthouse on Dearborn Street was scheduled to take place on a Thursday. My heart and soul told me not to go, but I knew that he would be very disappointed if he didn't see my face that day. My family was well aware of what was going on. My sisters, brothers, and father were the first point of contacts that I made to explain the incident. They would eventually hear about the robbery anyway since it was all over the news and social media, but I wanted them to hear the news from me. Many of my friends reached out to check on me but in actuality they wanted to know what was going on with him and the robbery. This added to my anxiety and depression because never in a million years would anyone associate me with a person who would make such a selfish move as he did, simply out of greed.

After speaking with my older brother, he agreed to accompany me at the preliminary hearing and be my moral support. He worked at a high school not too far from my job. We met at my office so that we could walk over to the courthouse, which was about a 15-minute walk. I was so happy that he agreed to go with me because I was terrified of going by myself. I was fearful of the unknown as it related to my son's future. I didn't want to see him, but I knew that I had to. When we arrived, we had to pass the security screening before going to the assigned floor. I didn't know where his case would be heard. My brother and I were able to locate the information on the kiosk that was in the lobby. It directed us to go up to the 23rd floor.

There we waited because we were a little early for the hearing. I scanned the lobby looking for his public defender. She told me that she would call upon her arrival to the courthouse. The lobby started to fill-up with news stations, reporters, and what seemed to be federal agents assigned to the case. The reason I was familiar with his situation and the court process was because I just went through the very same thing over a two-year period while he fought his other cases between California and the State of Illinois.

At exactly 1:00 pm everyone who was waiting in the lobby started to go into the room for his hearing. I decided to wait in the lobby to give them some time to get situated. My brother and I walked in the courtroom last and all heads turned and looked at us. They wanted to know who we were, and I'm sure they assumed that we were there for him. The back door opened and the sheriff told all to rise. The judge walked in and took his seat. The rest of us in the room did the same. The back door opened again and while the case docket number was read in front of the courtroom the sheriff and Charlie walked from the back to take their seats. He was shackled in chains with limited mobility or assistance. My heart skipped a beat as a result of me seeing him for the first time since the robbery. I was nervous about everything that was happening in that moment. When he saw me, he nodded his head at me and sat down. When he did that all heads turned around and looked at me, they were interested in knowing who I was and the nature of our relationship.

The preliminary hearing was very quick. His bail was denied as expected and his next court date was established. The sheriff got back up to assist and they all headed to the back to the chambers for his transition to the Metropolitan Correctional Center located in the heart of downtown Chicago. Afterwards, I briefly met with the public defender to discuss what would happen next. Everything that she stated to me, I expected. I knew that it would be an open and shut case because of the severity of what happened and the fact that he got caught in the act of a robbery.

When he got up, he made sure that he got my attention by hitting the left side of his chest with his fist, which meant that he loved me. I waved and said that I loved him back and he exited the courtroom with the sheriff right behind him. My stomach dropped, and my eyes immediately started to tear up. My reality set in and this time was very different than the previous cases that he fought. I grabbed my brother's arm because I was so overwhelm and he told me that everything would be okay. When I exited the courtroom, the lead federal agent for Charlie's case approached me. He wanted my contact information and I wasn't sure if I was supposed to give it to him. I looked over at my brother for confirmation and he insisted that I did because I had nothing to hide about anything. So I proceeded and gave the agent my information in which he told me that his office would be in contact if need be.

The reporters were in the courtroom to voice record the details of the case because it was the most recent and hottest story to report on that occurred over that weekend. What my brother and I weren't prepared for was the cameras and television stations that had set-up shop in the lobby of the facility. When we got off the elevator with his public defender, the reporters start to approach us and we immediately retracted our steps and went an alternate route to exit the building. In addition, I put on a pair of sunglasses to avoid anyone taking my picture to use for their benefit.

Chapter 7 – Mentally Preparing for Bid Number 2

All the events that took place over that weekend were déjà vu for me. The bank robbery brought me right back to the mindset of anger and confusion. I was right back in the same situation with Charlie, but this time it was worse. This time he would have to spend an extensive amount of time in prison. This time would be different because we had a son. Evan was a week into turning six months old. This time I knew, but couldn't accept that my life was about to change. My life as I understood it at that moment was over. In hindsight, I felt like the events that took place needed to happen in order for me to get in a better place in my life. I grew tired of the secrets, lies, and dishonesty that were the foundation of our relationship. The shift began from life with him to life without him.

He was able to call me after a week of processing back into the federal system. Everything was already established as far as my information being on file to receive calls and visit him at the same MCC facility because of his previous case. I received a letter in the mail detailing how sorry he was for what he had done and that he would fix everything for our family and things would be okay. He always knew what to say and how to calm me down during bad times. When he was able to call me, the conversations were very awkward. I didn't know what to say to him at all. I was angry, withdrawn, and depressed. He started off the conversation by apologizing for what he did but he assured me that all would be well. All I could say was how could you do this to us? I wanted answers and he didn't have any for me. He was adamant about me coming up there to see him in which I was a little apprehensive about doing because of what happened.

At that point, I realized that I wanted to be done with our relationship. I also felt bad for him because he had no one else to reach out to that would be able to assist him financially and emotionally during that time. I felt obligated to take care of him to the best of my ability, even though he did the crime and was put in jail as a result of his actions. He made statements that he needed me and he couldn't move forward without me. He pleaded for my assistance to help him with everything that he needed on the case.

I committed to making a trip twice a week to visit him in prison. We would talk about his case and how he wanted to go to trial with it. He planned to dissect everything including his capture to identify a way to get out of the situation. He was not going down without a fight and that concerned me because I was expecting him to take full accountability for what he did and apologize to the people that were involved and worked in the bank. For almost two years, I made the sacrifice to the visits, without hesitation. I sent him money on a bi-weekly basis and there was money always available for him to make phone calls to me whenever needed. I was accessible to him. I recommitted myself to being in a relationship with him even while he was in jail. He convinced me that we were in it together and I needed to give him an opportunity to make it right. I wanted my family back and I was hopeful that one day our nightmare would go away, so I agreed to stay together and get through that hard time.

We had everything mapped out. I would visit on Wednesdays by myself and Sundays were considered to be our family day with Evan who was six months at the time and didn't have a clue to what was going on. Evan was still very familiar with him and knew that Charlie was his father. Our visitation routine would continue while he would go back and forth to court fighting what everyone thought would be an open/shut case for all parties involved. This type of behavior and mindset was very typical for him. He was very, proactive, convincing, manipulative, and could articulate any plan that he had roaming through his brain. He was creative, therefore, nothing would surprise me when it came to him. His primary concern was getting home to his family by any means necessary. It was written on his face and it didn't matter what he said or who could possibly get hurt as a result of the determination for him to come back home to us.

The more that I begin to visit him twice a week, the more confident I became with entertaining the idea of him returning home. Subconsciously, I knew at bare minimum he would have to do ten years in federal prison. I figured that he would have to do eight years of that to be eligible to come home and Evan would still be young enough to still know his dad and want a relationship with him. I had it all mapped out in my head about how things would play out, but morally and spiritually there was a disconnection that I kept avoiding.

He still had complete control over me mentally and emotionally. Despite the severity of what he had done, it was still not sufficient enough for me to move on. I felt desperate to get my family back, obligated to stay with him and get through the hard times, and overwhelmed with emotions that I was unable to deal with as a result of his decisions. He never acknowledged the fact that I was truly hurting on the inside. He would say things insinuating that I was very strong and he doesn't know how he was blessed to be with a woman like me. I felt like I needed to play the role in which he forced me to play. He never knew how I dealt with the trauma happening internally.

I continued to make sacrifices to visit him every week. I would even stop paying some of my credit card bills to insure that I was able to send him money as well. The monthly amount was between $100-$150 that would cover the phone calls and commissary for him to buy food on a daily basis. This made me feel like I didn't have a choice but to comply with his every demand. He said that he needed my assistance, and I wanted to prove that I could be the strong woman that he needed to be by his side, again. It didn't matter what I thought or how I felt in those moments. He expected me to honor his every request and get things done no matter what. I didn't have a choice, and I couldn't say no. It felt like I, too, was incarcerated, but instead of being physically away from my world, I was emotionally and spiritually in a different place of no return. I became the very woman in the visiting room with my son that I vowed never to be. I shunned those women during his first time in a federal prison. I pondered how they could allow their children to see their father in an orange jumpsuit and shackles incarcerated. There I was in the same situation where I, too, was awaiting my visit in the same lobby area. My son Evan was very young at the time and he lacked patience to deal with the long wait and lengthy process of getting on that elevator to see his dad on the 23rd floor of the building.

I wanted it all to be over. In his presence, I played the part of a strong black woman who was ready for anything. Behind closed doors, I was stressed out about being a single mom. I was depressed about my life, my one bedroom apartment, and the fact that at times I couldn't afford a $20 can of Similac for my son. I was scared and became full of anxiety at the thought of moving back home with my mother where everything in the neighborhood was a reminder of poverty. I screamed one day that I wanted it all to stop. I wanted to make the noise in my head and pain in my body to stop, but it didn't. It was my reality. It was my new normal way of life. I continued to push through being a single parent to my son because his father made bad decisions in life. I really wanted to ball up in my bed, turn the lights off, and wish that my circumstances were different. My family helped me out consistently with my son. Whether it was financial or moral support, the help went a long way. My son, Evan was the motivation to keep moving on despite how it looked. I didn't know how, but I felt like my situation would get better eventually.

    His case went to trial after a few months. No one could understand why he would risk getting more time by going to trial for the robbery. I tried to convince him to change his mind on numerous occasions, but he did not. He was adamant about taking a risk to have his case go to trial. The motion was submitted by his lawyer to the courts and approved by the judge. In his mind, he wanted to risk it all to have a fighting chance to get back home to Evan and me.

Trial meant the preparation of evidence and witnesses on both sides. The employees at the bank that were tied up would have to rehash their accounts of what happened that day. Evidence would have to be examined by federal labs that included a gun with an extended clip. They would also need to speak with me because the lead attorney and his team thought it would be a good idea to use me as a witness. I was investigated with great detail including the federal agents coming up to my job to find out if I was really at work. It was very uncomfortable and embarrassing for my colleagues and direct supervisor to see me being indirectly involved in that situation. I sat in my office that day in disbelief of what was happening right in front of my eyes. I refused to speak with the federal agents without a lawyer because I felt like my constitutional rights were being violated. It seemed like as a result of my refusal, they decided to come up to my job in an attempt to get some information regarding my timesheet from my direct supervisor.

    I was called to the federal office on Dearborn Street to speak with the prosecutors who wanted to prepare me for trial. Everything happened in one week. He was then ready to push forward with trial. The leading prosecutor on his case wanted to interview me for trial preparation. He told me that it would only be a minute with him. I complied and left work early that day to attend the meeting. After a brief wait for the prosecutor to come out, he appeared with a couple of agents and a note-taker. When I saw that, my anxiety heightened yet again. I was under the impression that it would only be the prosecutor and myself going through some questions that would be presented. What started off as a pretrial preparation turned into an hour-long unconstitutional investigation about everything that he was involved in.

The prosecutor on the case brought up everything from potential kids that he may have hid from me to the number of women that he was involved with as a result of them dissecting his cell phones. I was shocked at the information presented and hurt by learning about other children that I had no knowledge about. I'm sure the interrogation was designed to get me upset, so I could tell everything that I knew about the robbery and his lifestyle. There was nothing for me to say because I knew absolutely nothing about his plan to attempt to rob one of the biggest banks in the nation.

I sat at the table overwhelmed with fear. At one point, I thought they were going to put me in jail just for knowing him. It was constant questions that were fired at me from so many different angles. At one point, I was almost in tears because, once again, I never thought I would end up in this situation. How did my world drastically change overnight? After two hours, I was finally released from the room and was told that I may be called on the stand to testify for the prosecutor and the defense.

I quickly gathered my belongings and headed directly to the elevator without looking back. I decided to go back to work and finish up my day. I wasn't present in that moment. My mind was very cloudy and I was confused as to what to do next. I wanted the voices and the events that were taking place in my life to stop. All I wanted to do was get back home to my son and figure out my life.

Trial began the following day at the federal building downtown. I was a witness for both sides, so I wasn't allowed in the courtroom to watch the progression of trial. Instead, I waited outside in the lobby area of the courtroom for a few hours. While I sat there, all I could do was meditate on life and everything that was taking place in my world. It's like I was asleep and having a nightmare that I couldn't get up from it. The day that I was there was the very last day of trial. After a few hours, the entire prosecution team left the courtroom and headed to the elevators to leave for the day. I stopped one of the agents and asked for an update on whether or not I would be called. He told me that it was over and the jury had gathered to deliberate about the case.

    I felt relieved after hearing that news and excited to get out of the building and head back to work. I wasn't able to communicate with him during trial, but he was able to call me once he got back to the facility. I asked him how everything went and he said that it went well and he felt good about the outcome of the trial. It was a waiting game from that point on. We had to wait on the jury to return with a verdict about his case that only took a few hours. The jury found him guilty on the gun and robbery charges. I had no feelings and everything around me was at a standstill. Life as I knew it was over and I was having a difficult time accepting it, plus I was very afraid to move on to something different. The judge scheduled his sentencing to take place a few weeks after the jury found him guilty.

I continued my normal visitation schedule with him afterwards at the federal prison. It was awkward for me, but he told me that he suspected the conviction to happen and that things were headed in the right direction. I wasn't convinced that things were, but I continued to be hopeful of the best possible situation regarding the amount of time that they would give him for the convictions. He made sure that he said the right things to keep me around. He told me that on numerous occasions during my visits that he did not want to lose me. I still wanted to prove to him that I could be what he needed me to be in the toughest times because I felt like I was his wife. So, I waited patiently and with optimism that the tables would turn and mercy would show itself in the situation during his sentencing.

The sentencing day arrived and the case was set to take place at the same federal courthouse where his trial was held. I arranged to take the day off from work. I woke up that day not ambitious whatsoever about going. My son's daycare was about 10 minutes from my apartment, so I dropped Evan off early to head back home so that I could get ready for the sentencing. My heart was racing as my body filled with apprehension, fear, and insecurities. I decided to drink a bottle of wine to ease the anxiety. It was a bottle of

Chardonnay that was in my refrigerator. I drank the bottle in a matter of minutes before I decided to leave and head downtown. Driving my car intoxicated was the furthest thing from my thought process. The fate of the man whom I loved was in the hands of the judge and in a few hours I would know just how severe the consequences would be for us.

I stopped to pick up my parents from their homes and we headed to the courtroom. They prayed for me and uplifted my spirits with affirmations that God would take care of it. I had faith that all would be well but there was that wavering feeling in me of what if. I didn't overthink it and we continued to press our way to the federal courthouse downtown.

We thought the sentencing was going to be a quick process, but when they gave him the opportunity to speak, he talked for about three hours straight before the judge asked for recess. He decided that it would be a good idea to try and reason with the judge one last time before he got his time. I got an opportunity to speak to his character. In addition, my father spoke about my son Evan. The defense plastered a huge picture of Charlie holding our son Evan in the courtroom and it broke me down. Yes, I cried hard for my son and the hurt that he would have to endure because of his father's decision. It moved the courtroom and maybe the judge, but I wasn't sure if it was enough that he would get any time off of his sentencing. The judge decided to give the courtroom a break and we were to return at 4:00 pm to hear his sentencing on the case. What we thought would be a quick sentencing turned into another trial it seemed. I was due for a break anyway because of being intoxicated from earlier. At that point my head was throbbing and all I wanted to do was lay down. My parents and I decided to go to the nearby McDonald's for food that was five minutes away from the courtroom. As they conversed with each other, I sat there in complete disbelief and drunk which made me numb to my reality. My head was in so much pain from the alcohol that was in my system. I wanted the day to be done and over with. I was very exhausted and semi-depressed about my life and what we were going through. I wanted to wake up from the brutal nightmare and dark spiritual torture that I experienced.

We made our way back to the courtroom and stood up for the judge to enter from chambers. He told us that we could be seated and then asked Charlie to stand for the details of the sentence. After a brief description of the charges and the federal guidelines and specifics, the judge sentenced him to 35 years for the bank robbery and gun charges. The judge decided to max out his sentencing because he was considered a career offender. He was said to be a threat to society because of his actions on that day. The judge said that he wanted to make sure that he was a senior citizen by the time he was released and returned back to society.

The emotions in the courtroom were a relief on the side of the victims and shock to me regarding how much time he would serve in a federal prison. He always promised me that he would only do at most ten years for the crime and if he participated in some programs, he could shave off a few more years. I believed him when he told me that because it was exactly what he did with the state case years prior. I put all of my faith and trust in him and the outcome of the case. It was the reason why I stayed because the worst that could happen was something that I could deal with. It was light at the end of the tunnel and he knew that I would follow his lead.

He took the verbal persecution without fear or intimidation. He didn't blink or react as a result of hearing the amount of time he had to serve for the crime that he committed. Instead he smirked and held his head high before exiting the courtroom to head to his cell. He looked at me and whispered that everything was going to be okay, and I nodded in return. I left the courtroom and cried in the car with my parents who were there to support me. My life at that point was over and I fell into a deep depression as a result. My mind ran rampage regarding Evan and being a single parent. The feeling was so overwhelming and I couldn't emotionally or mentally take it.

    I broke down in the back seat of my car drunk and confused as to the direction my life would head next. I didn't want to speak to anyone about it nor hear advice as to what I should do. I started to blame myself for even making the conscious decision of bringing a child in a confused situation. I dropped my parents off at home, picked up Evan, and went back into an isolated state in my apartment. I was too broken to even pray.

Charlie called me immediately after the sentencing to talk to me about his time and as usually he told me that everything was going to be okay. He absolutely didn't want me to fret about the situation and he needed me. I was the closest thing to normalcy that he ever had. I was done hearing that from him. My confidence over time had diminished with him telling me that everything was going to be okay, even when I knew it would not be. My life was over and I felt like it was time for me to walk away from him for good. My spirit told me to walk away, but he still had complete control of my mind. He told me that telling him no was unacceptable in our relationship. I felt that I had to comply with his every request and command that he demanded from me. He used to tell me all of the time that I belonged to him and it was nothing that I could do about it. I continued to believe that. I dried my tears before speaking with him. I cleared my throat and asked what was next for us. Once again, I saved face for the sake of showing him that I can be faithful and true to him. The cycle of our relationship continued.

    The Federal Bureau of Prisons took a few weeks to designate him to a facility outside of Illinois. He was assigned to a maximum facility in Morgantown, West Virginia. It was a sad reality for me because I wouldn't be able to visit him anymore with our son every week because of the travel and money that would be involved in seeing him in West Virginia. I knew that it was time for me to make some changes in my life. I didn't know how I would move forward because we were together for over ten years and I was too embarrassed to ask anyone for help so I could restart my life in a different direction.

I had no clue what that direction looked like nor did I have any motivation to walk out by faith. There was no one I could turn to for an escape from the reality of my life. The stakes were high because my mental state and future depended on it. When he made his departure from the state, I started to see much clearer because I wasn't in the visiting room with him every week making turmoil and confusion seem normal. I was going through the motions alone with the comfort that he provided me within our relationship. It was time to surrender to The Most High or continue to follow Charlie.

I attempted to numb the pain with my sporadic alcohol use and partying at different clubs several times a week. I temporary took my mind off my world changing so rapidly. I wanted to make the noise and conversations in my head stop in order to live my life on a daily basis, but it seemed like I didn't have an escape out of what was going on at the time. The feeling of defeat and failure started to set in my spirit. My son was my only motivation that I could draw from because he needed me. Taking care of him and watching his growth and development was the highlight of my light.

When he wasn't around, I fell back into a depressive state that was emotionally torturing my soul to the point of no return. It was overwhelming and living my life without him was unfamiliar and scary to imagine. I didn't have the strength on the inside to walk away. Making a decision to walk away would be me walking away from my safe haven that he provided for me. It would put me in a vulnerable state of mind that I was unwilling to experience. I wanted things to be back to the way that they were. It seemed so much better than the way things were in my life.

So, I continued to visit with a smile on my face and hope in my spirit. The hope that God would have mercy on his sentencing and it would magically be reduced before he would leave the prison in Chicago. That didn't happen. I looked to him to provide some answers and directions as to what we were to do next. I listened to his reasons of why I should trust his word despite the heavy sentence the judge ruled on his case. He told me on numerous occasions how much he needed me to be strong and present during that time. It was almost like a guilt trip that he placed on me that I couldn't escape. He played around with so many different ideas that went against my morals just to save our family. It was his idea of helping but in actuality it was hurting our relationship and I started to become distant and disconnected from him.

    I didn't have the opportunity to deal with my emotions and thoughts as a result of his sentencing. I wasn't conscious of the depressive state that my mind had fallen into. Instead, I was forced to follow his lead no matter what. I had to adhere to his every direction and plan because, despite of him being in jail, he was still in control. I was internally crying for help and a way out of the spiritual torment that I was hiding. I couldn't talk about it to anyone, including him. I still loved him and needed him to fill those voids and tell me everything would be okay.

Chapter 8 – Breaking Free

Two years into the sentencing I still had consistent communication with him, he would figure out ways to make extra money to buy me a plane ticket to go and see him on occasion. We would exchange e-mails on a daily basis because he had to know what was going on in my life. He still commanded the respect of being my man and the father of our son.

I had to send provocative pictures on occasion to please his flesh because he couldn't see me weekly. Sending the pictures made me uncomfortable and out of my character, but I sent them anyway. I knew that I didn't have a choice, but I did it to remain obedient. Otherwise, I ran the risk of him getting angry with me. His anger turned out to be a full fledge verbal assault that eventually forced me to oblige.

I felt trapped and broken. He had me in invisible handcuffs. The very thing that I thought would help me break away from the relationship drew us even closer than we were before the bank robbery. I empathized with the fact that he didn't have anyone else to help him. I felt guilty that he wouldn't have an opportunity to see his firstborn regularly. I continued to be there for him even though I still couldn't help but wonder if the rumors were true about him having other children. Or did the prosecution make it up to get me to talk about what I didn't know about? I felt obligated to help out because of the things he had done for me throughout our relationship. My insecurities convicted me of my inability to move forward without him in my life. In my mind, he created me.

In return, he created a world around me that I was use to and desired. He painted a picture for me as if I never skipped a beat and it seemed authentic. I was impressed with the fact that he was able to still take care of us while being incarcerated. There were times he was able to pay bills, buy furniture, and send me on trips. He took care of our son by providing Evan with whatever he needed.

Every move for him was a strategic one and he knew the things he did for us mattered. I was a woman of routine and comfort and anything out the norm in my world brought about an uncomfortable feeling that I was unwilling to embrace. He was right. As a result of the moves that he was able to execute, I thought that things weren't that bad after all. It felt like I wasn't missing a beat because he helped us out on a consistent basis. I put my faith in him and his ability to create that comfort for us.

Eventually he was moved from the prison in West Virginia to another facility in Pollock, Louisiana due to his influence and relationship with other inmates and correctional officers. Before he left the facility in West Virginia, I took a flight to visit him, a flight that he paid for. There was something about this particular visit that was very different for me. When I traveled to see him out of town I was able to visit over the course of three days. I was happy to see him, but it felt like it would be the last time we would see each other for a long time.

    Nothing significant happened on that visit. We laughed as usual, ate lunch from the vending machine, and had deep conversations about our past and what we wanted for our future. After our three-hour visit, we stood up, embraced and kissed, and got in our assigned lines to go in different directions. We waved good-bye and I could read his lips as he told me that he loved me before walking out of the visiting room and back to his cell.

That visit was indeed the last time I saw Charlie and neither one of us knew it. He was very comfortable with the way our relationship was. It was like we never skipped a beat since the crime happened. Because I loved him and did everything he needed me to do as his woman and mother to his child, I made a decision to submit to him. I believed and trusted in him and his ability to make everything right for our family despite my spirit telling me to walk away. I knew that he would get himself out of the jam that he created because I witnessed him doing it before.

The idea of our reality changing never happened. Instead he spent the next few months creating ways to make money because he felt like that would make me happy and content with maintaining our relationship while he was incarcerated and even though it worked for a while, I knew that it would be short lived because of what I desired spiritually.

He proved to be a big help for me financially. Renting a condo wasn't cheap at $1800 a month. I had the assistance of his mother who lived with me, but things were still hard to manage with one income.

After a while, I started to gather more information from him to understand what was going on and how he was able to generate money from afar. I was not pleased with the information that I learned and it went against my morals and everything that I believed in. He poisoned people and risked others' lives just for the sake of contributing to my household.

Once again, I felt like the spirit of greed was starting to take over his life and everyone was collateral. I was too afraid to boldly tell him my thoughts out of fear of his response to what I had to say. I ignored my moral compass and held on to the fact that I was in love with him. The amount of time that we were in the relationship trumped everything else.

One day, after prayer and meditation on the direction that God was leading me to go into, I made up in my mind that I would not turn back and continued to move forward in my life, without Charlie. No matter how many times he called to verbally abuse me with his false accusations about what I was doing, I remained adamant about only engaging in conversation about Evan.

He made sure to throw into the conversations the things he had done for me. It made me angry and almost depleted my soul. It took me several years to come to a conclusion that I was ready to move on with my life and do something different for the sake of my sanity and spiritual progression. I knew that I was only giving The Father a percent of me because of a relationship that I couldn't let go. During that season, I knew that it was time to move on.

REFORM'D

It was time for me to make my departure from the relationship for good and act on it. I questioned myself as to whether or not I was willing and ready. He instilled so much fear in me and I didn't know if I was strong enough to leave. Our relationship had gotten to the point where he was dictating what he wanted done and how. I felt that I had no choice but to follow his rules because I was all that he had. He made sure that I knew that he didn't have family outside of my son and me. He always promised that he would make me his wife once the smoke cleared from his case.

In December 2016, I decided to take my walk serious with the Most High and let the relationship go. It was time for me to trust that God had bigger and better waiting for me. My spirit knew it, but my flesh was unsure of how life would be as a result of walking away. The Father showed me that all things would be transformed for my good. I knew that I just needed to trust Him and the process in which He destined for me.

I prayed for God to give me the boldness and faith that I needed to have the conversation with Charlie about parting ways. The idea alone gave me so much anxiety and conjured up fear within that I knew was totally opposite of who God was grooming me to be - *a reformed woman of God*. My next move would be my best and boldest move that I would ever make or consider in the relationship. I wanted OUT for good and to start a fresh life while pursing God. I knew that if I was obedient to the Father's will and not mine, it would be pleasing to Him and He would reward and bless me. I could pay it forward and help others spiritually, among other things. It was time for me to make that decision and no matter what, trust Him.

I explained my deepest feelings as we talked, but he wasn't open to my agenda at all to please Christ and live a great life. He accused me of being in another relationship with a man. His mother told him that I was staying out late and going out with other men. The truth was that I was getting closer to God. As I held my head down, I asked God to give me strength and let the words flow from my mouth.

    I held my head high and finally let the words flow from my spirit and eventually out of my mouth. It was time to end it all and this time I was prepared to never look back. Through intense conversations, threats, and pleads to come back in my life, I remained adamant about us not being in a relationship. Yes, he told me on numerous of occasions that he would take my life if I ever decided to leave him, especially now that he was back in jail.

    There was something deep down on the inside of me that gave me the tenacity that I needed to propel forward and trust the process. The Holy Ghost was working on my spirit and wouldn't let me go. It was an energy that I felt before, but was afraid to tap into it. In that moment, the feeling was stronger than it had ever been in my life. I was no longer in control of my destiny. It was in that moment that I realized my mind, body, and spirit needed to all be on one accord with God.

    My mindset was shifting because of my activity in church, prayer, and Bible study. I knew that I had to do the work naturally in order to start living a Godly life. It felt different. I began to feel vibrant and fulfilled. I grew hungry for that feeling to be a constant in my life. The conviction confused my spirit because I was still wrapped up in a soul tie with Charlie and loved him, but I was no longer in love with him. I didn't know how to break the soul tie. I begin to communicate how I was feeling, which I'd never done before and found out that it would take prayer and fasting, in addition to my spiritual activities to break the soul tie for good.

REFORM'D

The transition occurred when I experienced how mean spirited he continued to be towards me. I decided to casually date after five years of him being incarcerated. He was not happy about that at all. He tried to demean my character, tarnish my self-esteem, and inflict fear on my conscious. His words literally cut very deep. I was deeply hurt and sadden and he knew just how much. He knew how I felt about him and tried to use it against me. In the past, he would use his words to maintain control. The things that he said to me weren't indicative of someone who loved and cared for me. Otherwise, why would someone say such harmful things such as: "Tinka, I made you" and "you belong to me?" He wanted to make me feel so low that I would just give in and accept what he was giving me - as I had done so many times before. This time it was different. I needed to be firm with the decision that I made to move on with my life. This time my motivation was The Father and my beautiful blessing, Evan.

I knew that God broke the soul tie that was established for over 10 years. I was obedient with fasting and praying. Eventually, the breaking happened. God led me to boldly tell him that I was done with the relationship and as a result I felt a spiritual burden lift from my spirit. The feeling was so refreshing to my entire being. I felt liberated and free from the shackles of the relationship.

No more would I settle for being with someone who I was spiritually unequally yoked with. I was ready for the road of the unknown. My decision was worth it all. I finally knew what the feeling of being completely free felt like and I never wanted the feeling to go away. It was imperative that I live my life. Evan deserved the best version of me.

REFORM'D

I stopped having phone conversations with him by disconnecting the local phone number that was in place for us to communicate. There were no more naked pictures of me floating through the U.S. Postal system to the jail. E-mails were limited to communication solely about the well-being of our son, which eventually stop, too. He went from being angry at me to pleading with me to stay and work things out for the sake of our family. I was his only true support and active person in his circle. He didn't have support within his immediate family. That alone stopped me from leaving the relationship early on. I empathized with the fact that he didn't have a support system that he could depend on. My distance affected him, and he used every tactic possible to get me back. He even lied about having a heart attack and needing to be rushed to the hospital as a result. He made sure I knew how he felt about my decision through the numerous emails that he sent. It was inevitably stressful transition that I had to endure, but was needed to get the true blessings of The Most High.

No matter my decisions, good or bad, what saved my soul during a very perilous time was the spiritual foundation that was rooted in me through the word God. It was the very thing that kept my mind and helped me through the toughest moments in my relationship for over a decade. It was the reason why I never *fit in* with certain social circles when I partied at clubs. I knew at an early age that I was destined for greatness, but I had no clue what it was. The Father spoke to me through visions and dreams, as I went deeper into my prayer life. I regained my confidence and was reassured that God had a better plan for me. In Matthew 6:33 (KJV), The Father says, "but seek ye first the kingdom of God, and His righteousness; and all these things shall be added unto you". I went to church every Sunday and attended Bible study weekly. I wanted the word in my spirit so the work had to be done for me to sustain. Every morning I woke up at 3:00 am to simply pray and talk to God. It was my intimate time with Him. I desired to hear from Him. The Father gave me specific instructions on what to do and I knew that He wouldn't bless me until I walked away from the relationship in its entirety. He gave me the same vision earlier but I ignored it. This time would be different and I was willing and ready to do the work.

God knew exactly what He was doing and through my trials and tribulations He never took His hands off of my life. Even through the toughest and scariest moments of my life, I knew God had me. I have been in some risky situations because of my ignorance to another side of Charlie that I knew nothing about. I experienced The Father worked through his lawyer, a complete stranger, to help me before I almost went on the stand to lie in his defense. His lawyer warned me of the consequences of the decision I was about to make and advise me to really think about the negative impact that it would have on my life if I lied. Once again, The Father spared my life and showed me how even in my wrong He had my back no matter what.

I ran from God for over a decade by making the wrong choice, due to my curiosity of the fast life. Life was going too slow for me at 21, and I needed some excitement. There were some things that I needed and it wasn't happening fast enough. I ran from God despite His miracles, signs, and wonders that occurred in front of me. There were some instances in my relationship that I heard God's voice tell me to walk away. God had bigger, better, and greater things for me, but only if I chose to serve Him and not man. God wanted me whole-heartedly without doubt and fear. I avoided the signs from God, but something kept knocking on my spirit. It was an uncomfortable feeling at times because it was so powerful and I wasn't ready to receive it. I loved everything about the fast and carnal life that Charlie and I created. Through it all, God was speaking to my conscious to come to Him with all my baggage, losses, and pain.

    I knew that I was special to The Father. God allowed me to see miracles and He performed them right in front of my eyes to make me a believer. He put me in the toughest situations where I had done wrong only to bring me a fresh wind and show me that His grace is sufficient. It wasn't enough for me to surrender whole-heartedly to God's will because I didn't want to let him go. I looked at him as my provider, protector, and confidant for years, and I believed that I had gotten the best man out there. I felt that I didn't need anything or anyone else. I knew in my spirit that God wasn't pleased at all with my life or the direction that it was going in. I knew subconsciously that it would come a time that I would need to surrender my life to God.

The question always lingered in my mind of when I would leave. I didn't know what it would take for me to get there, but the shift in my life that God allowed me to experience, rattled my soul. When my son was born, I felt that my life was complete and we were in a good relationship. The birth of our child allowed us to get closer because we shared the experience of a miracle. Shortly after the birth of our first child, a sudden shift happened in my life that would change things spiritually. God gave me the blessing of bearing a child when the doctors told me that I needed assistance conceiving, only to be motivation for me to stay focus on the Father in preparation for what was to come.

When the bank robbery happened, my son was six months old. I made a promise to God while praying that if He would help me through the toughest season of my life that I would serve Him, establish, and keep a relationship with The Most High for the rest of my life. I didn't know where to go or how I would start the journey, but I knew with everything that happened, there had to be something more than what my life had come to. You see, the tingly feelings, visions, and reservations that I was experiencing in the beginning stages of my life were simply The Father blessing me with the gift of discernment. It was unfamiliar to me and scary at times. He kept me in situations that I placed myself in only to show me that His grace is sufficient and all that I need. Even though I was too blind to see what God had for me, I was still able to discern that God wanted me out of the relationship. He wanted me to honor and serve Him, not Charlie. I felt a tug at my spirit that was all too familiar, but my desires of the world felt too good. The alcohol use, partying, VIP treatment, and access to things pleased my flesh in the best way naturally, but it did nothing for my soul that needed to be saved.

In Psalms 37:4 (KJV) reads, "delight thyself also in the Lord; and He shall give thee the desires of thine heart." My desires of the world started to shift from material things to more spiritual needs and desires from God. I started to realize that despite the material things that I possessed, my soul was empty. I envisioned myself with a God fearing man who would study God's word and attend church with me daily. I imagined myself doing more with my kids because both parents would be in the home. The thought of such a life gave me hope for a better future. It made my soul smile, and I was ready for that life. I knew that life in the direction that I was going in was not indicative of Christ at all and He was not pleased with me.

REFORM'D

The Bible says in Exodus: 20:3 (KJV), "Thou shalt have no other Gods before me." The dynamics of my relationship put me in a position of complete surrender to my boyfriend. I idolized him because of what he could do for me, and I loved him for that. We had nothing in common from a spiritual standpoint and I was okay with gambling with my life to please him. I had no interest in building a solid relationship with The Father. I said to myself that believing was enough and The Father knew my heart. I went to church from time to time, but that's all that my relationship consisted of. I knew that what I was doing wasn't right, but I was willing to put my relationship with Christ on the back burner to please my flesh and my man. I felt like I had time to right my wrongs. I felt like the love and consistency of my behavior would get him to change for the better. The direction his life was going into wasn't indicative of the woman I knew God wanted me to be, but it was hard for me to let go.

I thought my anger and frustration upon Charlie's arrest gave me the courage that I needed to finally make the decision to walk away. It seemed as though God answered my prayer immediately due to the fact that I was stressed and overwhelmed with the cheating and inconsistent behavior. I asked God that if the relationship wasn't for me, to take it away. He didn't tell me how he would do it, but the unthinkable happened on the day of the bank robbery. I wasn't secured spiritually enough to walk away without looking back. God provided me with an opportunity to walk away and start a new life serving Him. The Father spoke to me through visions and dreams of how life would be if I chose to follow His plan for my life, instead of my own plan. I knew that I had to do it or my life would be chaotic and confused, especially for my son, Evan. It was time for me to live a fulfilling life that included God.

My next move would be my biggest faith move as I prepare to serve God. My mother helped lay the spiritual foundation for me. She made sure that I had a pulse rooted in the word of The Most High. In my moments of doing what I wanted to do, I reflected on the word and spiritual teachings that my mom embedded in me. Those reflections gave me the encouragement that I needed to push forward. I recommitted to attending church on a regular basis and not because I had to and was forced by my mother. My heart, mind, and spirit were ready to serve God with my every being. I found my church home through prayer. There I recommitted my life to God. It was an important step because I battled depression and isolation while leaning on my own understanding of what happened in my life. I absolutely didn't want to leave my one bedroom apartment with my son. I wanted to keep my eyes closed and hoped that it was a bad nightmare and it would go away once I woke up. I stayed in darkness and didn't like sunlight pouring into my living room. I was content in my space cuddling with my son literally all day because he was the only reason that I wanted to live despite the reality of my life.

    The enemy tried so severely to take my mind and kill me, but the blessing of my son saved my life. Seeing his face gave me comfort of hope and a better future through Christ. The responsibility of caring for his life gave me joy. At first, it was hard for me to pray because I didn't know what to say after being so disappointed with not only myself, but also a man that I was submissive to for over 10 years. The enemy attempted to trick me by way of emotional confusion and sporadic conversations in my head that life was over for me and telling me it was time for me to give up.

I knew that I had to give God a real try. What I was going through couldn't be life for me and it was time to try something different. The thought of starting over was scary, but I was confident that my life could get back on track.

After I surrendered to God, I knew that this time would be different. I didn't know how to live life on my own, but I knew that my first step was to surrender in order for God to move in my life. Even though my life was still in shambles, I felt God with me. I was in severe financial debt, filed bankruptcy, forced to be a single, first time mom to my son, I didn't have a reliable car because Charlie used my truck to commit the crime, and there was a possibility that I would have to move back home with my mother. I felt defeated and out of control and the outcomes of the decisions that I made in my relationship and lifestyle caught up to me, but I still knew God would get me out. For so long, I thought that I made things happen in my life and career. I experienced success in life because of the things I had done to improve my situation at work and school. I didn't have a road map of what to do as an adult, so I committed to figuring things out on my own which ended up being trial and error over and over. I gave myself all of the credit for my accomplishments in my professional life at the time. No praise was given to The Most High. But, this time, I knew only God would be able to get me out of my mess.

I learned that God desired the praise and glory. He proved Himself to be present in the most extreme times in my life. There were times where I felt like it would be over for me if I stood in front of a judge or federal prosecutors to lie for someone who I wanted to marry and spend the rest of my life with. The Bible says in Psalms 110:1 (KJV), "The Lord said unto my Lord, Sit thou at my right hand, until I make thine enemies thy footstool." This scripture resonated within my soul as I reminiscence on sitting in a room being interrogated by prosecutors regarding the case before trial. I felt helpless and scared for my life and freedom and I did nothing wrong. I felt like I was guilty by association and the prosecutors were coming after me.

All I could think about in that moment was my son and how I needed Jesus to show up in my life quickly. I remember sitting there with sweaty palms and scattered thoughts. I was irritated and defensive because I felt like I was tricked into being interrogated because of his decision to go to trial. Just when I was about to breakdown and cry, God showed up and saved me. One of the federal agents stood up and asked the federal prosecutor to step outside. I don't know what was said but when they returned to the room I was told that I could leave after being questioned for two hours. What was done to me was unconstitutional and illegal. God used my enemy to speak up on my behalf. Yet again, God spared me and showed me another miracle right in front of my eyes. At the time I didn't realize it, but after gaining a closer relationship with God he begin to show me all the ways that he saved me. I felt undeserving of it because I was making a decision to stay and commit myself to a man that wasn't following Christ and as a result of greed, left his family.

    I left the federal building in a hurry when I was told that I was free to go. As I walked down Dearborn Street in Chicago on my way back to work, I whispered the name, Jesus. I prayed and made a promise to God once again that I would serve Him with all my heart. I was ready to make things right in my life and God had to get all the glory because He is the One who saved me. Though it took me five years to act on my promise, all things worked together for my good. And here I

REFORM'D

stand walking in the will of God. I felt so special that God allowed me to see miracles and performed them right in front of me that day and there was no turning back at the point.

EPILOGUE

The impact of incarceration has impacted my son and me on various levels. My son, Evan is my world, but I had no clue how I would explain and justify the absence of his father to him. I told my son's father that I believed that was a conversation that he should have with Evan. I thought it would be right for him to hear it directly from the source, his father, as to why he was absent from the home.

When his father went to jail Evan was six months. He was too young to understand the things that were happening in our world. But, Evan knew who his father was and the moments that they shared. He still saw pictures and spoke with him on a regular basis before all forms of communication stopped with him. I dreaded the day that he would ask questions about him and the reasons why he wasn't in the home.

REFORM'D

As Evan became older and started school where he saw his friends with their mothers and fathers, he became curious about why his world was a little different. I was the sole parent dropping him off and picking him up to and from daycare and school. At the tender age of four, our son asked the question that paralyzed my spirit. "Mommy, when is my dad coming home?" I prayed and asked God to guide my words in order to give my son an explanation of what took place with his father. I felt compelled to, instead, have his father explain the reason why he was absent from his life.

I decided to allow Evan's dad to speak with him on the phone one day. I told Charlie that he needed to explain to Evan why he was no longer in his life. He agreed that he would and asked that I put Evan on the phone. Evan was excited to speak with him when I handed him my cell phone. Being able to communicate with him was the one thing that both Evan and I looked forward to daily before all communication stopped. It was how we stayed connected as a family. We spoke so much to him that things felt normal, but I was ready for a new journey of an abundant life following the Most High and having the conversation (between Evan and his dad) was another point of closure for Charlie and me.

Moving forward, I knew that my journey would entail some uncomfortable moments, but I was willing to go through them because I knew it would allow me to grow. I know, even now, there are still some things that need to be purged completely in order for me to operate in His complete purpose. But at least now, I am closer and closer to my destiny and reaching my full potential.

What I wasn't prepared for was the negative impact that the incarceration would have on my son. I was hoping that Evan would forget about his father over time. But I knew that he would start asking questions about his dad as he got older. In my mind, I had several years before that happened. Well that wasn't the case for him. He definitely remembered who his father was and asked questions about his whereabouts when he was only three years old. Evan would talk to him on the phone a lot to keep a relationship and bond with him. As a mother I was so desperate for that relationship to stay intact. It gave me comfort and hope that my son would be okay through this transition. I wanted to hang on to whatever I could in order to keep a sense of normalcy in Evan's world. It would break my heart to see my baby hurt over his dad being absent from the home. I felt like his life shouldn't have that unnecessary obstacle and it was my responsibility to shelter him from it as much as I could. I dreaded the day when I would have to sit down with our son and tell him that he wouldn't see his father for another 25 years. It built up so much anxiety inside of me and made me fearful of the future outcome.

In actuality, I was hurting my son by creating a false reality for him. The phone conversations and connections where not adding up to my son because he would ask me when was his father coming home. His dad initially told him that he was in the army and he would be home soon. My son continued to ask when he would be done with the army. I had no response to those questions.

During the conversation between Charlie and Evan, Charlie told him that he had done something wrong and as a result, he had to be away from him and wouldn't come home for a very long time. He was four when he had that conversation with him. Evan had nothing to say in response to what his dad told him. He gave me the phone and said that he didn't want to speak to him anymore because he had done something wrong. I was hurt and immediately comforted him and told him that it would be okay. My soul felt like it hit the floor because I could tell that he was hurt and that was the very thing that I wanted to avoid for so many years.

Evan is seven years old now and is still impacted by the absence of his father. There are moments of anger and rage that he has as a result of his inability to understand the void in his life. Those moments make me feel helpless. How does a mother explain to her child that their father won't be home for a very long time? I simply try to keep the communication open between Evan and I so he can express his feelings surrounding his father. I've noticed his conduct in school is affected and he would say it was because he misses his father and wanted to know when he was coming home. How does a mother respond to such a reaction from her child? I experienced so much anxiety because I wanted to protect my son from the very thing that he was going through in that moment.

As he gets older and sees his friends in two parent households or fathers walking their sons to school and basketball practices, his mind remains inquisitive as to his father's whereabouts in his life. The phone calls and communication have stopped between his father and me, due to me leaving the relationship. This is a personal choice and worked for our relationship. His biggest concern was not the well-being of our son. He wanted to rekindle and fix things with us in an effort to get back in my good gracious.

I could not go back to the way things were. I was excited about the opportunity to reform my mind, body, and spirit. It was time for me to live in my purpose without turning back. I didn't know what my purpose entailed, but it was time to trust in The Most High to assist me with discovering what that was. It was time to make changes in my life in order to reverse the generational curse that was already in place to work against my son, which was bad decision making and prison time.

"What doth it profit, my brethren, though a man say he hath faith, and have not works? Can faith save him?" according to James 2:14 (KJV). So the natural labor begins. It has been imperative for me to foster a village of support and male representation within my family and community for my son in place of his father's absence. I knew that a supportive village would help in his development. I knew there were some things that I couldn't give him as a woman. I have been leaning on family and friends to assist in this area. It's my prayer that he grows up to be a fearless man of God and world changer. In order for that to happen he has to know that it is possible. My village has been a great support with raising Evan because I can't do it alone, especially with gender specific issues such as: using the restroom, grooming, behavior, etc. It's a feeling of relief to know that I have a team who empathize with my son on this issue and are willing to help both my son and me. It's a feeling of relief and reassurance that, through God directing me, we will overcome any obstacle that lie ahead.

Charlie's absence has been a financial burden on me. The rising costs of school and other expenses that go along with having a child were overwhelming along with taking care of the household on my own. In addition, having one source of income by way of my job and expenses that exceeded what I was making created a very stressful season in my life. It was all on me to make things work. The lifestyle that he created for me was pressure to figure things out and try to keep up with what I had in the past. I had to make some tough decisions to survive on my own. It included sharing my residence and cutting back on expenses to stay financially afloat. I wasn't too keen on living with someone else because I enjoy privacy all too much. But, I had to.

It was a must that I keep everything as normal as possible, and I felt the sacrifices were well worth. Charlie made sure that I had more than enough when it came to cash on hand. There were times where I would easily have $20k in our personal safe at home. All of our bills were paid on time every month. I had no financial care in the world and my current circumstance was a shock for me. But now, that didn't matter to me because I wanted to earn money the right way for us.

Over the course of the past five years I became very angry. I had moments of rage because I didn't understand why he would make such a selfish move. I turned back to drinking daily to ease my mind off of my reality. It was clear that he didn't consider his family at all or the affects that it had on our relationship. The idea of being a single parent scared the life out of me. It brought me back to the way I grew up after my dad left the home and the affects that it had on my life as a teenager and young adult. I experienced my mother struggle with her children, especially emotionally. She, too, battled depression and it left a bad image in my mind of being a single parent. I had to deal with Charlie committing the crime. This was the reality of my world and it scared me and sent me into a state of shock and depression, but God healed and delivered me.

I lived my life on a set routine in an abnormal relationship. There wasn't a rule book to give me step-by-step instructions on what to do as a single mom. Getting things done was all up to me. It was up to me to become a successful single parent, despite how bad the situation. The reality was that Charlie was no longer around. He was no longer there for me to lean on or to help me. I not only had to break out of depression and thrive in my reality, I had to become a great mother and successful professional. But how does one do it?

I had to reach deep down inside to find my soul in order to release it back to The Father and live a purposeful life under His statues and commandments. I needed God to help me with the reformation of my life. I didn't desire to do it on my own. I tried and it didn't work for me. There was no way that I was going to figure it all out either. But once I began to chase The Father for guidance, the new journey became clearer and has been great thus far.

Leaving my son's father was one of the hardest decisions I had to make. It was difficult because I had to abandon a life I knew and start over with sole reliance on The Most High. The decision made me fear the unknown that I had no control over. Questions started to surface in my head as to my next move regarding housing and other important factors in my life. I prayed and had an open and honest conversation with God. He gave me a peace of mind and reassurance that I was making the best decision for my son and me. I knew that if I didn't turn from my wicked ways, my life would be filled with turmoil and confusion. My life depended on my shift.

There were moments where I wanted to remain content on the status of our relationship. I felt that I owed my son's father my loyalty and respect because of the things he did for me. But when I reverted back to the thought of getting back with him, I immediately prayed to God for help and strength during my most difficult moments of vulnerability.

I choose to take it one day at a time without prejudgment and regrets. I won't say things are perfect in my life now, but I love the direction that it is going. Often times, people ask me "Tinka how did you get through so much so suddenly?" To be honest, I still don't have an explanation of how I got through the toughest time in my life because it wasn't me that got myself through it. I can't take the credit for healing my mind from a depressed state due to fear and anxiety. There's no way I've been able to raise my son on my own. I can't take the credit for raising such a boy who is growing up to be an amazing young man. I give all the praise and honor to The Father and the Son for helping me in the most difficult time in my life. There were so many moments where I felt like giving up and I was on the verge of accepting the reality in my life.

There were dark thoughts that attacked me on a daily basis regarding my son and how his life would end up because of who his father is. I still think about the potential void that my son would feel as a result of an uncontrollable factor in his life.

Rather than embrace that my life had seemed to change for the worse because of what Charlie did and the loss that I experienced, I pray and go deeper for revelation of what The Father is doing. In Jeremiah 1:5 (KJV) it says, "Before I formed thee in the belly I knew thee; and before thou camest forth out of the womb I sanctified thee, and I ordained thee a prophet unto the nations." I did not choose God. He chose me. He knew of the choices that I would make in my life, the men that I would date, and the direction my life would go in. He strategically set it up that way, so I could make a choice between chasing my salvation and falling victim to some bad decisions. Otherwise, why am I still living and breathing? I had no choice but to embrace what happened in my life. As I go deeper in the word of The Most High, my faith increases. It's a wonderful feeling and I wouldn't stop this direction that I'm going in for anyone. There's no turning back now.

REFORM'D

As I sit in my room at my mother's apartment, my spirit is full, and my mission is clear. My temporary circumstances are not a damper to my faith whatsoever. The season is uncomfortable but it will soon change and will continue to get better. I have witnessed signs and experienced miracles behind a catastrophic event that happened in my life. It was supposed to kill me and take my mind. The enemy had a plan, but The Father's mission was bigger and greater than I could ever imagine. The pain wasn't for me, it was for the woman suffering with a husband or significant other currently going through the prison system.

You're not alone in your journey. There are so many women who are suffering, depressed, lonely without family or friend support systems. You're not alone and don't be afraid to speak up about what you're going though. I thank God daily for keeping my mind through the reformation of my life to live for Christ committedly. Nothing else matters right now and I count it all joy. The pain truly has brought purpose in my life surrounding women and children suffering from the effects of the mass incarceration of African America men. The repeat offenders who unfortunately don't learn from lessons of hardship must stop. Our men are falling victims to the systematic epidemic that exist in our society. What can be done? Is it too late? How do we take back the impacted households and overcome the systems that have existed for decades that don't help, but hurt our loved ones?

Through my experiences, a transformation of my mind and spirit had to take place immediately. There's no other way it would have worked. The generational curses must stop and our children will not fall victim to it. I took my way of thinking out of the equation and didn't depend on my own understanding to move forward in life. Just as I made the decision to submit to a man, I'm now submissive to The Most High. I don't want to control anything again in my life. The Bible says my plans aren't His plans - therefore, I have chosen to follow The Most High and chase my salvation now more than ever. It has truly been an experience as my life transforms right in front of me. The restoration process has taken place in my life and it has me saying, *that was nothing, but God*.

What if all women affected by mass incarceration made the decision to restore their households and submit to The Almighty? Think about the positive impact it would have on children and the men who fall prey to such a system. It's a choice and a spiritual one that will change everything around you. Are you ready for that? Can you handle the purging of all things that aren't aligned with His will? Are you strong enough? Does your heart desire something bigger and better? It's not easy, but The Most High is faithful. It's time to lead by example in our households, especially for our children. Our seeds need to be the motivation to move forward and do better.

There's an old saying, the grass is never greener on the other side. Well, I beg to differ. The grass is definitely greener on the side with The Father, The Son, and The Holy Spirit. My life is an illustration of His grace, mercy, love, and kindness that has rejuvenated my world. Overflow and restoration in every facet of my life has manifested from a full turnaround in my finances and a promising future. It's exciting and humbling experience that God took me from where I've come from to where I am now.

If you are in a relationship that you know is not connected by God, get out. Move on and move forward. Allow God to work miracles in your life. Allow God to bring you peace, love, and joy. I'm excited about your reformation and your future because of the spiritual work you've decided to do. This journey is nothing short of amazing!

STATISTICS

One out of every three African American boys born during this time can expect to be incarcerated during his lifetime according to alarming rates and statistics. The NAACP stated, "African Americans constituted 34% of the total 6.8 million correctional populations in the United States alone". Mass incarceration in Black communities is an epidemic that is plaguing so many families, including wives and children. But are we really speaking up on the issues and the impact of loved ones falling prey to a *system* in America? Why do our men not only fall prey, but become repeat offenders in the prison system?

The statistics is what it is but why aren't the women who are affected by this epidemic speaking up? Why aren't there support groups available where women of all ages and walks of life could receive support and encouragement? Why isn't the true reformation of our communities happening on a daily basis? How can we take back our communities and set the right example for our children while taking back our households?

TINKA RANDLE

www.ingramcontent.com/pod-product-compliance
Lightning Source LLC
Chambersburg PA
CBHW071945110426
42744CB00030B/301